OUR DAVY

When the news arrived from India of the gallant but unfortunate action of '80 against Hyder Ali in which Captain Baird was engaged, it was stated that he and other officers had been taken prisoners and chained two and two. The friends were careful in breaking such sad intelligence to the mother of Captain Baird. When however, she was made fully to understand the position of her son and his gallant companions, disdaining all weak and useless expressions of her own grief, and knowing well the restless and athletic habits of her son, all she said was:

"Lord pity the chiel that's chained to our Davy."

Dean Ramsay.
SCOTTISH LIFE AND CHARACTER. 1860.

OUR DAVY

General Sir David Baird, KB.
1757 – 1829

by

Arthur H. Haley

BULLFINCH PUBLICATIONS

Published by
BULLFINCH PUBLICATIONS,
245 Hunts Cross Avenue,
Woolton, Liverpool L25 9ND.

Produced By
THOMAS LOUGHLIN,
Mulberry House, Canning Place,
Liverpool L1 8JG.
Tel: 051-709 0818/9

Typeset By
TYPEBASE LTD,
1 Marybone, Liverpool L3 2BT.
Tel: 051-236 0601

British Library Cataloguing in Publication Data.
Haley, Arthur H. (Arthur Henry), *1912 –*
Our Davy: General Sir David Baird, KB. *1757 – 1829.*
1. Great Britain, Army. Baird, Sir David, *1757 – 1829*
I. Title
355.3'31'0924

ISBN 0 9511427 4 7
ISBN 0 9511427 5 5 pbk

For Barbara

CONTENTS

ACKNOWLEDGEMENTS

I wish to express my thanks to the following for providing access to sources on which the book is based.

Tom Hartman for supplying me with the loan of T. E. Hook's *Life of General Baird*.

British Library.

Public Record Office.

Ministry of Defence Library.

National Library of Scotland.

Scottish Record Office.

Scottish United Services Museum.

South African Library.

Government Archives of South Africa.

University of Nottingham for the loan of a Thesis on *Lochie's Academy* by T. A. Bowyer-Bowen.

The Institute of Oceanographic Sciences, Bidston Observatory for estimating the time at which George Napier delivered the message from General Moore to General Baird.

Liverpool Central Library for assistance with my researches.

The many individuals who replied to my requests for information.

ILLUSTRATIONS

The portraits are reproduced from *British Soldier Heroes* (1898) by Spencer Wilkinson.

MAPS AND DIAGRAMS

INTRODUCTION

David Baird stands out as a rare example of an 18th Century soldier who, with little patronage or wealth, attained the rank of general in the British army by his own efforts. He has been depicted by most of Wellington's biographers as volatile and bad tempered though for this they produce no evidence. In an age when duelling was prevalent he was never called to fight one nor is there any record of his ever having been involved in a personal quarrel.

One of his many friends, Sir James McGrigor, Wellington's Chief Medical Officer in the Peninsula and later Director of the Army Medical Service, served with Baird in India and Egypt. He writes that Baird's life was so full of adventure as to be 'more like romance than history' and describes him as 'at all times firm and influenced less by alarm than any man I ever met'.

By a vagary, not uncommon in history, Baird's reputation has been shadowed by two fortuitous remarks.

His mother, on being informed that her son was a prisoner of war in an Indian gaol and chained to another officer, remembering his restless and athletic habits when a boy and being determined not to show her grief in public, all she said was:

'Lord help the chiel that's chained to our Davy.'

The second is attributed to the Duke of Wellington by J. W. Croker, the society diarist:

'Baird', said the Duke,' was a gallant, hard-headed officer', but he hand 'no talent, no tact', had an unpredictable temper and by past experience was unfitted to govern the natives.

The Duke's opinion has been accepted by most of his biographers without reservation. Other writers, however, have regarded his comments as coming from one who had reason to be biased and that, except for his gallantry, Baird's character was the opposite to that stated by the Duke.

In this book I have set out to narrate the dramatic adventures in which Baird was engaged and to give an objective view of his character, not only as seen by those who served with him from high ranking officers to private soldiers and the people of India, but the impression he made on those with whom he came into contact on the fields of battle and in the seats of power.

Arthur H. Haley.

BAIRD

CHAPTER 1

Early Life

The fifth son of an Edinburgh merchant, David Baird was born on 26th December 1757 at Newbyth, a mansion house in East Lothian. A few years later his parents moved with their increasing family to the Gordon House, a large stone building near the top of Castle Hill in Edinburgh, a move which was to prove of lasting importance to David, for it can hardly be doubted that his formative years in the crowded Old City helped to fix in his mind the strong character traits which marked his career.

Like all the dwellings then providing shelter for Edinburgh's 70,000 inhabitants, the Gordon House was divided into apartments with various grades of society packed under the same roof, maiden ladies on slender means, artisans, shop-keepers and servants filling every nook and cranny of the building. In this tightly knit community, where all were interested in each other's business, exchanged greetings on the stone stairways and jostled in the narrow streets and closes, young David was initiated into a robust, convivial and uniquely democratic way of life, soon to be swept away as Scotland emerged from its isolation into the modern world.

The Baird family continued to increase annually until David was eight, when his father died leaving his mother to raise seven boys and seven girls. That all survived at a time when the majority of babies entered the world only to expire mysteriously as by an act of God, may be taken as proof of an unusually sound heredity. It is also possible that growing up in 'the dirtiest city in Europe', its streets used as open sewers where pigs were allowed to root amongst the garbage, David acquired an immunity to diseases for which there were no known cures.

His mother, Alicia Baird, was a prime example of what Henry Cockburn cited at the end of the 18th Century as a 'singular race of old Scotch ladies, who stood out like primitive rocks above ordinary society'.* Ambitious for her childrens' success in life, she adhered to the traditional rules of child management that would today be regarded as inhuman.

Refraining from all shows of affection lest she should weaken their characters for the trials that lay ahead and with a dour sense of humour making light of their troubles, she looked after their health according to the nostrums of the day and punished their mis-

*Memorials of His Time, 1830.

demeanours with a sound whipping or confinement in a room on bread and water.

David appears to have given her most trouble. Undeterred by punishment, he displayed all the determination to follow his own dictates that would bring him into conflict with authority in later life. Nevertheless, her influence on him was profound and at some stage a mutual understanding must have been reached, for he always looked back on his childhood as happy and on his mother with affection. He was fond of repeating how she used to sing the old Scottish ballads. When he obtained the command of his Regiment, he had the tunes transcribed for the band exactly as she sang them.

At school, like many another high spirited lad, he failed to see the relevance to his own life and aspirations of the Classics which then filled the curriculum and, regardless of the routine flogging, neglected his studies.

The Bairds were of Highland descent, with a proud military tradition dating back to the Middle Ages. And although the Lowland branch, founded in the reign of Charles I by James Baird, who came south from his home in Banffshire to study law, had been most noted for its lawyers and merchants, there had also been merchant adventurers who sailed to America and the Far East, and soldiers who served with distinction in the English and Dutch armies.

The Gordon House stood only a few yards from the Castle entrance and, as a child, David was fascinated by the sights and sounds from the garrison's parade ground, (now the Esplanade). When this was followed by 'restless and athletic habits and an aversion to schooling', his mother was left in no doubt that 'Davy was born a soldier'.

At a time when commissions were purchased and traded like any other commodity, raising the sum required would have been difficult for a younger son in so large a family. For David the problem had been solved by the untimely death of his eldest brother when, with a prior claim to available funds, he had been on the point of starting a military career. The commission purchased for him was retained and with this still bearing his brother's name, David was gazetted ensign in 2nd Foot (the Queen's Regiment) on 14th December 1772, a few days before his 15th birthday.

Like many another young Scot, he was moving out of a closed community into the more permissive society of an expanding world of exploration and Empire. His formal education was slight and his outlook narrow compared with most of the young gentlemen with whom he would associate. On the credit side he possessed a sharp intelligence, a splendid physique and complete confidence in himself.

His entry to the Army was unusual. Instead of joining his Regiment he took his place as a cadet in a Military Academy run by Louis Lochie, a refugee from the Netherlands which was then occupied by the Austrians. Lochie, who had given much thought to the training of soldiers, had been shocked to find that any 'gentlemen' could buy a commission and promotion in the British Army with no test of his physical, mental or moral fitness. His system of officer training, set down in a long Essay on Military Education, was more than a century ahead of his time.

On Baird, the parts that were to make the greatest impact and which he was later seen to act upon, were that both officers and men should undergo strenuous physical and mental training to prepare them for the hardships of a campaign and that officers should carry out their duties as meticulously as they expected the men to do.

An indication that he was prepared to put the theory into practice occurred soon after he arrived at the Academy. He was on sentry duty when an older cadet approached and when challenged said that being a senior he was not required to produce a pass. Baird replied that he had not been told of the privilege. His orders were to allow no one out without a pass. The cadet again stressing his seniority added that, being a new boy, Baird must be ignorant of the way things were done. Never one to engage in futile arguments, Baird suggested that as the cadet was so senior he should be able to knock down a very junior recruit and walk out over his body. Nonplussed by this unexpected proposition from the newcomer who appeared so confidently in charge of the situation, the cadet sized him up and returned to his quarters muttering dire threats.

After a year at the Academy, Baird joined his Regiment at Gibraltar. He had learnt more about his profession than many officers would in their whole careers. Yet, when it came to promotion or selection for commands, his knowledge would count for little. His contemporaries who rose to eminence - men like Wellington, Moore, Hope, Graham and Craufurd - were, at his age, moving in the social and political circles where the power lay. But Baird had either no interest in these sources of power or was not yet fully aware of their importance.

He arrived at Gib four years before Lord Heathfield was sent to organise the Rock's defences for the Great Siege and, as he soon discovered, they were in a sorry state with guns fallen from their mountings, parapets crumbling, moats filled with rubble, ammunition and stores run down. Warnings by successive commanders, that unless repairs were put in hand the place would be indefensible, had been ignored by the Government. Senior officers had lapsed into cynicism leaving the whole garrison demoralised.

There could hardly have been a worse spot for an enthusiastic young ensign to start his career and the first few weeks proved a testing time for the 16 year old Baird. His determination to carry out his duties was at first viewed with amusement by some of the more time-serving subalterns who decided to make him late for guard inspection. He had dined and was about to leave the room when one of them locked the door and took out the key. No stranger to pranks of this sort, Baird made for the window, dropped the considerable distance to the parapet and went on to inspect the guard.

At the end of the three years he arrived home on leave to a joyous reunion with family and friends. His return was also well timed for the advancement of his career. The American War of Independence had begun and the depopulation of the Highlands had turned them into a fertile recruiting ground for the Army with the Clan Chiefs being encouraged to form their own regiments. Among the Chiefs so engaged was Lord McLeod of the Mackenzies, a supporter of the Stuarts in the '45, who had just returned from self-imposed exile on the continent where he had served in the Swedish and Prussian Armies.

Most of his officers were members of his Clan. But the fighting qualities of the Highlanders, the romantic aura with which their past was being invested and the growing unity between North and South brought a flood of applications from the Lowlands. David Baird, now an imposing 6 feet 3 inches, broad shouldered, well-proportioned and athletic with strong regular features, steady grey eyes and the confident look of command was accepted, promoted to lieutenant and on his twentieth birthday, made captain in the grenadier company. The promotion was a godsend for, being in a newly raised regiment, it was free of purchase. He had been in the Army five years, long enough for a young gentleman with the necessary cash and patronage to have advanced to the command of a regiment. But for him the £2,000 or so required to buy a captaincy would have been out of the question.

Among his fellow officers were his boyhood friend James Robertson, a son of Principal Robertson, the historian, and the brothers John and James Lindsay whose sister, Lady Anne Barnard, has left in that curious collection of contributions from the family, *Lives of the Lindsays,* a graphic account of childhood under their tyrannical mother, Lady Balcarres. John, soon to become a close friend of Baird, she describes as 'pleasant and eccentric, respecting neither rules nor persons.' When a plaything was taken from him for doing something for which his mother rebuked him the day before, he said:

"Woman, I told you I would do the same and I'll do the same tomorrow."

Tomorrow came, he kept his word and was whipped. But the sun shone brightly and he said:

"Ah! Here is a fine day and my mother cannot take that away from me."

While regretting that their mother never showed them any affection, Lady Anne, no doubt speaking for most children of the Scottish matriarchs of her time, admits that she taught them "those general rules of equity and honour, of mind and truth" which continued to guide their behaviour through their lives. She was a woman "to make men of boys and wise women out of silly ones".

Without doubt Baird found the ethos of his new Regiment more congenial than the 2nd Foot. His stay at Gibraltar had given him experience of the normal regiment. He was now returning to the customs and values of his earlier years in their most esoteric form - the mores of the Highlanders.

While the average soldier was ruled by fear of punishment, the Highlander was motivated by the customs and traditions of his forefathers, instilled into him from infancy. The worst that could befall him was to bring disgrace on his family by breaking the code of his clan. Being under the continual scrutiny of his fellow clansmen, news of any fall from grace would be sure to get back to his people. This would bring the ultimate punishment. He could never return to his home and community.

Unlike the average loud-mouthed, drunken soldiery, he was conditioned to being cautious in his dealings with others. In clan warfare, the slightest insult had demanded redress or revenge, imposing on each member the need to control his speech and actions lest he should bring disaster on himself or his clan.

Until Governments introduced a policy of recruiting outsiders, flogging in Highland regiments was practically unknown. Physical punishment would have destroyed the Highlander's pride and rendered him useless as a fighting man. His blood relationship with his chief had conferred the right to discuss matters that concerned him. Anyone who aspired to lead such men had to share their traditions and assume the role of chief. For this reason nearly all the officers were Highlanders with a few selected applicants from the Lowlands.

Baird would spend more than twenty years with the Regiment. After his boyhood in Old Edinburgh, his year at Lochie's Academy and three years at Gib, those years would set the seal on his character and have a decisive influence on his conduct and the decisions he would make in the years to come.

His first task was to recruit men of good character from Edinburgh and the surrounding districts. When the Regiment assembled at Elgin in the Spring of 1778, the muster comprised 850 Highlanders, 236 Lowlanders with 36 English and Irish. The inclusion of 'outsiders' was not fortuitous. The Regiment would have to function with others and as the Highlanders spoke only Erse, a leavening of English speaking men was essential.

A few weeks later orders came to march the 600 miles from Fort George to Portsmouth to embark for India. Arriving to find no ships ready for the long voyage, they sailed to Jersey to repel an expected French invasion. It failed to materialise. They returned to Portsmouth and for the rest of the year were dispersed in billets over the surrounding countryside, hardly able to communicate with their unwilling hosts and regarded as little more than savages. Early in January 1779 they were marched on to ships of a large fleet in Portsmouth harbour where they remained cooped on board for two months. On 7th March, almost a year after leaving their native Scotland, the fleet sailed.

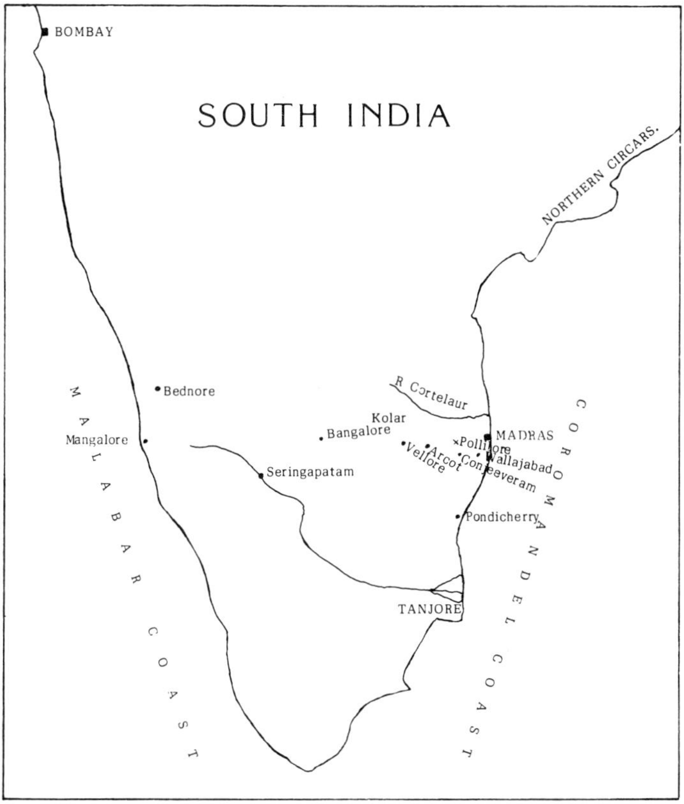
BOMBAY
SOUTH INDIA
NORTHERN CIRCARS.
Bednore
Mangalore
R Cortelaur
Kolar
Bangalore
MADRAS
Pollilore
Vellore
Arcot
Conjeeveram
Wallajabad
Seringapatam
Pondicherry
TANJORE
MALABAR COAST
COROMANDEL COAST

CHAPTER 2

India. Battle of Pollilore. 1780.

On the long voyage to India, disease could decimate a regiment as effectively as a campaign. Yet thanks to stops at Madeira and Goree and a three months stay at the Cape where they were put ashore to assist the civil authorities, McLeod's Highlanders arrived at Madras in remarkably good shape. The ships dropped anchor in Madras roads at the end of January 1780 and they were ferried ashore in the marsula boats before a crowd of 50,000 curious onlookers assembled on the beach to see for the first time 'the soldiers in skirts'.

The Highlanders' joy at reaching their destination was short-lived. They had been buoyed up with promises of what to expect on arrival. Their living quarters would be better than any in England. They turned out to be a two storied building 'like a Portuguese convent', last used as a granary, its walls black with grime. The soldiers accommodated on the ground floor and the officers above had first to drive out the rats and mice that infested the place.

They had been promised pay and allowances equal to those of the King's forces in Bengal. The promise was not honoured. Baird, like other officers on small means, was reduced to near poverty by the convention that required him to employ a number of servants according to their rank.

A more crushing blow was to fall. Continual attacks by the ubiquitous mosquito reduced the Highlander to 'a miserable object with his face swelled over his eyes in bumps like smallpox and ulcers in his legs that did not close for weeks'. The change to white drill trousers was resisted until so many men were incapacitated that the Regiment was unfit for combat. The kilt was abandoned.

While these setbacks gave rise to the soldiers' natural outlet of grumbling, a groundswell of rumour began to revive their spirits. Hyder Ali of Mysore was about to declare war on the British and drive them into the sea. The rumour was denied by the Government. But the natives were in an obvious state of fear. Talk in the Army turned to prize money, batta, (double pay for officers on active service) and promotion.

The consternation roused by the name of Hyder Ali is understandable. This remarkable man, though illiterate, had risen from obscurity to become the ruler of his Country, had vastly extended its borders and had evolved by his genius all the trappings of a military state. Unique among Indian rulers, he realised that no native army, however large, could compete against trained and properly equipped European units. Using the British as a model, he had enticed Europeans and sepoys to train and lead his forces, had adopted British drill and uniforms, had orders given in English and even had military bands playing British martial music.

Soon after coming to power, he had sought friendship with the British. But since 1772, when the Madras Government had broken a treaty of friendship by refusing to come to his aid when he was attacked by the Mahrattas, he had found other allies and nursed his resentment. In the Spring of 1779, with irony which he would not have failed to relish, he had drawn his old enemy, the Mahrattas, into a confederacy aimed at driving the British into the sea. With the French at war with the British, he could also count on their support and advice.

He had made no secret of his designs, yet it was January 1780, just before the 73rd arrived, that the Madras Council took steps to counter them by sending reinforcements to the Circars (the coastal strip to the north of Madras) and ordering the enlistment of more sepoys into the Company's army.

A few weeks later, the Governor, Sir William Rumbold, sent in his resignation to the Directors in London on the grounds of ill-health, at the same time assuring his successor, John Whitehead, that all contingencies had been covered and that the British had never been stronger. Few believed him. When he sailed for England on 6th April, the gossip columnist of the *Bengal Gazette* observed with sarcasm that the departing Governor was reported not to have accumulated a very large fortune. 'It was little more than £600,000'.

A month later, on the pretext of performing ceremonies at his father's tomb, Hyder moved part of his army to Kolar, close to the Carnatic border. In June, Colonel Lang, Commandant at Vellore, sent an urgent warning to the Council that the whole Mysore army was assembling for an attack. They brushed aside the warning.

Later that month, Hyder marched his army from Kolar to the Pass of Changama. His grand total of more than 90,000 men included 50,000 infantry (of whom 15,000 were trained in the European system), 28,000 horse, 12,000 auxiliaries and 400 French. He had also a peculiarly Indian weapon - elephants trained to advance on the enemy flailing 6 yards of heavy chain and trampling all before them.

Early in July, with all his troops in place and his spies having reported no enemy activity, Hyder gave the order to advance. His vast army debouched on to the Carnatic Plain, moving to a carefully laid plan. Kureem Sahib, his second son, with 5,000 cavalry, drove south to Porto Novo which it proceeded to sack. Another division under Tipu, his son and heir, headed north to cut off the British in the Guntur Circar. Hyder himself advanced to Conjeerveram and prepared to lay siege to Arcot.

Other cavalry units fanned out and began to converge on Madras, pausing only to destroy all traces of human habitation and round up the wretched villagers with their flocks and herds ready to be driven back into Mysore. Their approach was signalled to the inhabitants of Madras by pillars of smoke rising in all directions. Then appeared the straggling groups of terrified refugees who had managed to evade their pursuers.

The Madras Council, its dream of invulnerability shattered, turned in desperation to Sir Hector Munro, the C-in-C, who, from his past record would appear to be just the man for the crisis. For, by a decisive victory against overwhelming odds at Buxur in 1764, he had established British power in Northern India and won the reputation of 'a daring, dashing warrior, ready for any enterprise however foolhardy'.

But that was sixteen years ago and certainly foresight does not appear to have been one of Munro's attributes. Although the forces at his disposal were adequate, it was only now he realised that they were strung out in perilous isolation over more than 400 miles of the Carnatic Plain: at Trichinopoly, Colonel Cosby with 2,000 men; at Pondicherry, Colonel Brathwaite with 1,500; in the Guntur Circar, Colonel Baillie with 2,800 and at Madras the main army of 5,000 that included the 73rd, the only complete European unit.

He at once sent orders to the various commanders to converge on the Presidency with all speed and the main army to assemble at St. Thomas Mount, four miles south of Madras. Within a few days he could expect to have a powerful army at his disposal.

But now fate, in the form of an urgent plea from the Nabob of Arcot, intervened. His capital was surrounded by Hyder's forces. He called for the Madras army to march on Conjeeveram to force Hyder to raise the siege. Supplies would be no problem; Arcot could provide all that was needed.

Munro, experienced in Indian diplomacy and warfare, and with full knowledge of the record of the Nabob's duplicity, seems to have accepted his appeal without hesitation. He instructed McLeod to march on Conjeeveram and sent orders to Baillie, already on his way to Madras from the Guntar Circar, to change course and make for the same destination.

McLeod was astounded. He pointed out that the only safe place for the two forces to unite was Madras. Conjeeveram was forty miles away and an open town. The Madras army had neither the equipment nor supplies for so hazardous a venture. For Baillie to march on Conjeeveram would add many miles to his route and take him into the heart of enemy held territory. On the other hand, if he kept to his present line of march he would be in Madras in two days. Only when the two forces were united and adequate supplies collected, would he (McLeod) be willing to lead the expedition.

"I have been many years in the service", he concluded, "and I have always observed that when you despise your enemy, he gives you a damned rap over the knuckles."

McLeod was obviously in the right. But it was Munro who had to make the decision and make it quickly. With the lives of thousands of men, the fate of the whole army and even of the British in Southern India in the balance, he appears to have been determined to prove at all costs that he was right and McLeod was wrong. After persuading the Council to appoint (illegally) another member in his place, he announced that he would take the field at the head of the army.

Up to this point, feeling sure that, with Baillie so near Madras, Munro would make no move until their junction had been effected, Hyder continued to concentrate his forces round Arcot and even recalled Tipu's cavalry from the north.

Then on 25th August, Munro began his march to Conjeeveram. His force, strengthened by a detachment from Pondicherry, numbered 1,800 Europeans and 5,000 sepoys. They had a bare eight days' provisions and advanced through a countryside of blackened villages and crops with Hyder's cavalry hovering menacingly.

For the Europeans, new to the Indian climate, the merciless blaze of the sun proved an even greater threat. Man after man fell at the roadside to drink the stagnant water. In three days the lives of 200 soldiers were lost, chilling the hearts of their comrades and adding to the air of foreboding.

On 29th, Conjeeveram was sighted. As they approached the town, a large body of horse bore down on their van as though about to attack. Turning instead, it rode back into the town and was seen soon after leaving on the far side. At the same time smoke and flames began to rise from the town's centre.

Of Baillie there was no sign and, equally important, the need for provisions was becoming urgent. A representative of the Nabob had accompanied the army to arrange for a large quantity of rice and 200 sheep to be made available. The man now blandly informed Munro that he had received no such instructions. Aware at last of the trap into which he had been led, Munro wrote desperately to Governor Whitehead for supplies.

A few hours later the threat of immediate starvation was lifted. By pushing rods into the ground and smelling the tips, the advance party discovered stores of grain buried under the streets. These were dug up and stored in the pagoda where they could be defended. Though the amount was not large, the grain and its defence was to play a decisive part in the course of events.

Hyder, having been fully informed by his intelligence of the location and strength of the two British forces, began to raise the siege of Arcot and place his army between them. At the same time he despatched his son, Tipu, with large bodies of cavalry, infantry and artillery to intercept Baillie.

That officer, upon whose judgement the fate of so many would depend, had already been faced with one important decision. On August 25th he had arrived at a small river, the Cortelier, almost dried up. For security he decided to camp for the night on the north bank. When morning broke, the river, fed by the mountain rains, had swollen to a raging torrent. To cross was out of the question. A week later, still unable to move, he sent a message to Madras asking to be allowed to proceed to the mouth of the river and be transported there by sea. He received no reply.

On 3rd September, after a delay of nine days, he was able to ford the river and resume his march. On 6th at Perhambaukam, still 14 miles from Conjeeveram, he made his first contact with the enemy. Tipu's cavalry, though greatly superior in numbers, circled and threatened, while his artillery began a three hour duel in which they were worsted. He then withdrew and sent for reinforcements.

For Baillie it was a pyrrhic victory. He had lost 100 men and expended much valuable ammunition.

Munro, meanwhile had clearly heard cannon-fire and rightly deduced that Baillie was under attack. Conscious of the need for action he gave orders to strike camp, and, placing his heavy guns in the pagoda, marched towards the firing. After proceeding three miles he came upon Hyder's army, massed to dispute his progress. He halted and for the next three days remained facing the enemy. On an open plain, without tents, exposed to the burning heat of the sun, his men suffered greatly while the effect of the inaction on their morale was even more disastrous.

On 8th he received a message from Baillie, written in Erse in the absence of an agreed code. After recounting the reasons for his delay and the engagement with Tipu, his closing sentence ran:

"I cannot come on. I am in want of everything and expect you with anxiety."

Had Munro been the man he was at Buxar, he would have thrown all into the hazard and broken through the massed forces of Hyder. But with age and good living had come caution. His duty to relieve Baillie was balanced by the need to protect the supply of grain. To advance with his army would place the pagoda in the hands of the enemy. To detach a force strong enough to defend it would destroy his chance of driving through to Baillie.

In desperation he did what wisdom should have advised when at St. Thomas Mount. He called a council of his field officers. After deliberation it was decided to send 1,000 of their best troops - ten companies of sepoys with the grenadier and light companies of the 73rd commanded by Captain Baird and Lieutenant John Lindsay. Colonel Fletcher, in command of the force, was ordered to tell Baillie to rest his reinforcements for a few hours then march on Conjeeveram. Munro would march to meet him half way.

The relief party set out in the evening of the same day. Hyder, whose spies were everywhere, immediately sent a strong force of cavalry to intercept it. But Fletcher, suspecting the loyalty of his guides, consulted Baird, his second in command, and decided to change his route. At dawn they sighted Tipu's camp less than half a mile away, the men asleep and unguarded. Rarely can such an opportunity to destroy the enemy have presented itself to any side in war and had not Fletcher been specifically warned against such a venture, he would certainly have ordered an attack.

Regretfully, the march was continued. At 7 a.m. Baillie's force was sighted across what appeared to be a lake but on investigation proved to be the outflow from a tank, the sides of which Baillie had cut to strengthen his position by flooding that side of his camp. Having covered 20 miles in the night the relief party now had to wade through a wide stretch of water to join their comrades.

Still, with the re-formation of their forces, there appeared better hopes of the two armies effecting a junction, always provided their leaders acted with resolution. Baillie at least wasted no time. Allowing his reinforcements a few hours' rest he resumed his march at 8 in the evening.

For six miles his route ran through open country under continual harassment by Tipu's cavalry and artillery. He then came to a road lined with banyan trees that led into a jungle. After proceeding five miles he ordered a halt for the night. The reasons he gave were the fatigue of his men, the panic among his camp followers, who, as in all

Indian armies, outnumbered the fighting men by about eight to one, and his ignorance of the state of the ground or the position of the enemy.

His caution, though understandable, was, none the less, his second major error of judgement. Fletcher, whose intuition throughout seems to have been sound, protested strongly against stopping, but was over-ruled.

Sound too was the intuition of Tipu. Seeing the British settling down for the night, he withdrew his forces, sent to inform his father of the situation and began to deploy his units ready for morning.

Hyder, continuing to watch Munro closely, consulted his French advisers who warned against him being caught between the two British armies. But reading the situation more accurately, he arranged by messengers with Tipu the plan to be put into operation the next day. Then, maintaining his position until 4 in the morning to be sure that Munro was preparing no move, he set his army in motion in the direction of Baillie.

At daybreak, Baillie resumed his march. After two miles he came to the end of the jungle and could see the road running between two low ridges to a village about 1,200 yards ahead. With no enemy in sight and without the precaution of sending forward his scouts, he marched towards it.

When half the column had emerged into the open, volleys of grapeshot suddenly burst upon them from batteries behind the left ridge. In an attempt to regain the protection of the trees, Baillie ordered an about face, at which firing was opened up by a battery hidden in the woods to the right. He turned his column again and attempted to resume his march on the village, until, finding himself under fire on all sides, he called a halt and ordered his gunners to engage the enemy. They did so with such effect that he told off two companies of sepoys under Captain Lucas of the Company's army to take the enemy guns. As the sepoys advanced the gunners fled.

A mass of cavalry had meanwhile appeared from behind a screen to Baillie's right. They charged but at 40 yards were met by such concentrated fire that the leaders fell and those behind were forced to turn and run the gauntlet of the British line, to be brought down in scores. Reaching the end, the survivors wheeled to attack the rear guard. Beaten off they turned again to cut off the sepoy detachment that had arrived at the enemy guns. The cry of 'horse' went up and the sepoys ran back in panic to the main body, leaving the guns intact. As the cavalry fell upon them with terrible slaughter the enemy gunners returned to their guns.

Up to this point the action had been in the open. Baillie now, belatedly, moved his men to a dried up water-course leaving his gunners to continue their duel. The enemy were again forced to leave their guns and as the whole enemy fire began to slacken and their infantry to withdraw, it seemed that with the expected arrival of Munro, victory would be assured.

An hour passed. Then the familiar strains of 'The British Grenadiers' were heard and all eyes were on the clouds of dust billowing out of the village. Column after column of red-coats appeared and a great cheer swelled up from the beleaguered army. Just as suddenly it died away. The columns were fanning out and reforming for the attack. Hyder's army had arrived. Within minutes the plain was swarming with his infantry, cavalry and artillery.

Baillie gave the order to form a hollow square and fire from the prone position. The enemy closed in on all sides until they were firing into their own ranks. Then came wave after wave of cavalry, to be repulsed with losses so terrible that the onslaughts began to waver. Even at this late hour victory seemed possible.

But now fate struck its most cruel blow. Two of the tumbrils exploded, killing the gunners to a man. The camp followers burst in panic through the ranks of the soldiers. Many sepoys who had matched the courage of their European comrades tore off their uniforms and fled. The few remaining British, together with the sepoy officers, reformed. But Baillie, realising that further defence was useless, tied his handkerchief to his sword and raised it, calling upon Baird, now second in command, to cease firing.*

One of Hyder's officers called out that if they laid down their arms they would receive quarter. But whether from confusion or to avenge their enormous losses, the cavalry led by Tipu charged in for the kill. The British remnant picked up their arms and fought on.

> "— impenetrable bodies of horse, infantry and artillery advanced on all sides like the waves of the sea --- clashing of arms and shields, snorting and kicking of horses, snapping of spears, glistening of bloody swords and cries of bruised and mutilated men, wounded horses tumbling to the ground upon expiring soldiers and the hideous roaring of elephants stalking to and fro and wielding their dreadful chains alike amongst friends and foes.
>
> "Such as were saved from the immediate stroke of death were so crowded together that it was with difficulty that they could stand; several were in a state of suffocation; whilst others, from the weight of the dead bodies that had fallen upon them were fixed to the spot at the mercy of the furious foe."

*Colonel Fletcher was already dead.

Among the last to fall was David Baird. Throughout the battle he had given his orders to his company who, to the amazement of the French onlookers, had carried them out 'with as much precision, coolness and steadiness as if on the parade ground'. After the explosion of the tumbrils he had fought on with his sword into the final onslaught to fall at last with two sabre cuts on his head, a ball in his thigh and a pike thrust in his arm.

During the night of the 9th, Munro had made preparations to march at daybreak in the direction of Baillie. At midnight he heard the sound of guns but, after a while, the firing stopped. Soon after daybreak came heavier firing and, at the same time, he saw that Hyder's army had disappeared. He marched towards the firing on the right of the road along which Baillie was expected. After four miles he fired guns to signal his approach. Minutes later he heard an explosion and saw a column of smoke rising. The firing then ceased and he returned to the main road hoping to meet Baillie.

McLeod had all this time been anxious to march with all speed. He now begged Munro to do so. Being refused, he pleaded to be allowed to go ahead with his Highlanders to assist their comrades. This too was refused.

When the army had marched another two miles, a wounded sepoy appeared with the news that Baillie had been overwhelmed. More fugitives began to arrive, telling dreadful stories of the atrocities committed by Hyder's men.

Deciding his only course of action was now to look to his own safety, Munro returned to Conjeeveram only to find that the store of grain he had been so determined to defend, now amounted to little more than one day's supply. Ordering his heavy guns to be thrown into the tank (reservoir), he began his retreat to Chingleput where he hoped to find provisions.

Under continual harassment by Hyder's cavalry, symptoms of demoralisation began to appear in many units, signalised by 'a straggling fire without object, the strange but ordinary effect of panic'. Aided by this breakdown in discipline, the marauding horsemen were able to pick off 500 men in three days' march to Chingleput. There, Munro's hopes of finding provisions were not realised but, joined by Colonel Cosby's contingent from Trichinopoly, he made his way back to Madras.

Why, it may be asked, did Hyder allow Munro to escape?

It would seem that he too had become cautious with age. Throughout his engagement with Baillie, he had been apprehensive that Munro would arrive on the scene. As soon as the battle was won, he removed his army from the field and did not immediately follow Munro, who was given a few precious hours' start. When he did begin the pursuit, his orders were to harass and not to start a battle.

CHAPTER 3

Captivity in Seringapatam 1780-1784

In the first glimmer of returning consciousness, Baird perceived the figure of a native soldier towering above him. Attracted by the movement of his eyes, the man was raising his spear to strike. At the same instant, by one of those quirks of fate that decide the fate of individuals, another wounded soldier groaned. On him the spear descended and the executioner moved on.

The reprieve might have seemed a small mercy. Wounded and dead were now a prey for the scavengers of the battlefield. One of the human kind had already stripped Baird of all but his blood-stained shirt and trousers. Jackals, hyaenas, vultures and kites had moved in for the feast.

As consciousness increased, the searing heat of the sun and a raging thirst drove out all other sensations. He lay for an indeterminate space of time until at last he discerned a horseman draw near and kneel beside him. His head was raised and a few drops of water trickled down his parched throat. He was lifted to his feet and assisted slowly and painfully away from the stricken field. With the exertion, blood from his wounds began to flow and he fainted.

The soldier waited for him to recover then they set off again. But after a second and a third attempt the man, who had evidently been hoping for the reward offered by Hyder for all British prisoners brought in, realised his task was hopeless. He did not vent his disappointment on his fallen enemy. Perhaps touched by the sad state of one of his own fraternity, he left him to his fate.

Baird was now alone. But the unknown horseman had removed him from the dangers of the battlefield and probably saved his life. He lay in a twilight of consciousness until he became aware of two figures walking towards him. A sergeant and a private of the 73rd, they were overjoyed at finding one of their own officers. Both were wounded but managed to give him water, raise him to his feet and support him in the supposed direction of Munro's camp. Their progress was painfully slow and at last the three sank to rest in the shade of a banyan tree, where Baird slept soundly for several hours.

When he awoke, his companions told him they had seen Tipu's cavalry go past, evidently in pursuit of Munro who must either have been defeated or was retreating to Madras. Now able to think more coherently, Baird decided the only chance to escape death or imprisonment was to make for the French camp. He indicated the direction

HYDER ALI

they should take and by good fortune they reached their objective before nightfall.

The French received them with kindness, dressed their wounds and gave them a meal. But as their spirits began to revive, their captors, who had not the heart to tell them at first, now said they could not remain under their protection. Hyder had given strict orders for all prisoners to be handed over to him personally on pain of severe punishment.

Next day they arrived under escort in the enemy's camp just in time to see Baillie with a number of officers coming out of Hyder's tent. Delighted to see John Lindsay among them, Baird called out but was not at first recognised. In Lindsay's words:

"A figure covered all over with blood came limping up to me and called me by name, which, from the voice, I soon discovered was my old friend David Baird. This was a most welcome meeting for both of us."

Though less severely wounded, Lindsay had had a remarkable escape. Pinned under a pile of dead and dying, he had received a stab wound from a pike that passed through another soldier. He had tried to bribe a horseman to take him prisoner. After taking his money the man had stripped him of all but his shirt and trousers, slashed him with his sword and left him. His life was saved by the French standing over him with their drawn swords.

He told Baird that Hyder had received them with relish, gloating over their wretched condition. But when Baillie retorted that, as Hyder well knew, his victory had been due to the ill-fortune of the British and not by his army's prowess, Hyder, who never allowed emotion to cloud his judgement, noted Baillie's defiance and, changing his tone, brought the discussion to an end by ordering the prisoners' names to be taken and telling them with menacing irony to go to their quarters and 'eat, drink and be happy'

That night 58 officers, more than half severely wounded, were herded into a tent. Scraps of food were thrown on to a cloth in the centre and they were told by the guards to eat or starve. Two French surgeons came but treated the wounds of only the worst cases.

By the morning three prisoners were dead. The rest were told they would have to march to Arcot before receiving medical attention, - a typical ploy by Hyder to encourage them to cooperate. Many protested they could not march, some of them even falling to the ground and taunting the guards to kill them. All to no avail; the march began with only the most crippled like Baird carried on doolies - rough palanquins of bamboo bound with coconut fibre.

After two days the stench from the prisoners' wounds so filled the air that the French officers were moved by compassion to petition Hyder for help. To satisfy his allies he allowed each prisoner a piece of cloth to cover himself and Baillie was given 2,000 Rupees to buy food and necessities. This he divided equally among officers and men so that each received 5 Rupees.

Their condition continued to worsen. Herded at night into a tent pitched in the street, they had to lie on the bare ground, making it impossible to prevent dirt from entering their wounds. Death came daily and the stench from their wounds at last became so overpowering that the natives refused to come and sell them food.

On 16th September, Hyder sent most of the prisoners to Mysore but kept Baillie and seven officers including Baird and Lindsay at Arcot. They were allowed to say farewell to the men of their companies who had been longing for the chance to complain of their treatment. Finding their officers equally helpless, they burst into tears and could only console themselves with the hope that the day would come when they could avenge all their sufferings.

Baird was now immobile from his wounds that had become infested with maggots. A request was made to Kistnarow, Hyder's chief minister, to ask the Commander at Vellore, who was only 16 miles away, to send them a surgeon. Kistnarow replied that if they had so much influence over the Commander they should ask him to surrender the fort to his Master. When they indignantly refused, he told them to expect no more favours from him.

This incident proved a turning point in their attitude to their captors and a boost to their morale. For, in hope that Kistnarow would make their lot more bearable, they had been subservient. They now began to treat him with studied contempt. Those able to stand no longer got up to salute. They even thought up ways of holding him up to ridicule.

On 22nd October, all the officers except Baillie were told to prepare for the 200 mile journey through the mountain passes to Seringapatam. Although those unable to walk were carried on doolies, the long journey added to all their sufferings. Their money ran out and was not replaced. They had to travel in the heat of the day. They were fed only in the evening after the guards had eaten and had a sleep. At night they were held in cowsheds from which the animals had been driven out.

By the 27th John Lindsay had lost his power of speech and in spite of Baird's efforts to feed him, was unable to eat. Yet now occurred an incident that helped to restore their faith in their fellow beings. One

PLAN OF THE PRINCIPAL PRISON OF SERINGAPATAM

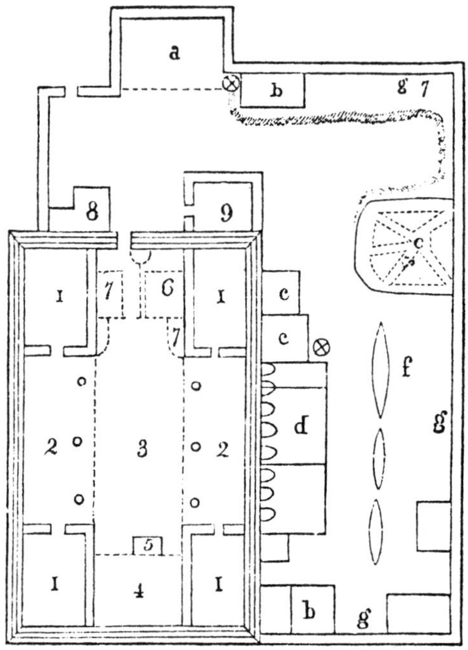

1. Corner Rooms, each containing 4 cotts.
2. Verandas matted off, each containing 7 cotts.
3. Inner Yard.
4. Old Cook Room containing 6 cotts.
5. Mr. Massy's Kitchen Garden.
6. Sied Ibram's Berth.
7. Pyals.
8. Sied Ibram's Cook Room.
9. House.

a. Hospital, 2 cotts.
b. Collery Guards.
c. Servants' Huts.
d. Prison Cook Room.
e. Captain Baird's Garden.
f. Old Mud Walls.
g. Mud Wall, 18 feet high.
h. The Outer Door of the Prison.

N.B. Each corner room of the Prison about 16 feet long by 10 feet wide.

of the guards told Lindsay he would prepare some medicine for him if he would take it. Lindsay indicated that he would but that he had no money to pay for it. Saying he wanted none, the sepoy produced three pomegranates and some sour milk. He mashed the pomegranates with a stone and mixed them in the milk with his hands.

In other circumstances Lindsay would have rejected the concoction with loathing. Now, in spite of the horrid taste, he drank it and soon fell asleep. He woke a few hours later and, for the first time in five days, Baird was able to feed him with a little boiled rice.

When the guard came the next morning, Lindsay thanked him for saving his life. The man was overjoyed. Lindsay told him that although he now had no money, he had plenty in his own country and would reward him when he was free. The guard drew out his little purse and, saying his pay was a pagoda a month (about 60p), he offered Lindsay a rupee. Lindsay expressed his deep gratitude but refused it; overwhelmed with this unexpected kindness he burst into tears.

On 30th October, at a village called Pripatam, the guards made a little money on the side by putting the prisoners on show; the villagers paid gladly to see such strange creatures. All were in rags, some had their heads shaved with a piece of glass to keep down vermin while others, like Baird, had gaping maggot-infested wounds. The simple audience had many a laugh at their grotesque appearance.

After 16 days on the road the party arrived within sight of Seringapatam. Though Baird's wounds were still open, Lindsay's were quite healed. He believed this was due to the shortage of food, for he had received no treatment for them at all.

Seringapatam was built on an island formed curiously by the River Cauvery separating and joining up again. On sight of it the guards started jubilantly pointing to the high walls of the fort where the prisoners would be held, stressing the impossibility of escape.

They were ferried across the river and escorted through excited crowds to the parade ground in the fort, where they were lined up a respectful distance from the Kellidar (Commandant) and other dignitaries seated to receive them. Presently a servant came to ask if they were enjoying their stay in the Behadur's territory. From weakness and dejection, they said, to the amusement of their audience, that they were. When this humiliating ritual had been repeated for several hours in the heat of the sun, they were led away.

The prison building was set in a compound 100 feet by 70 feet, surrounded by walls 18 feet high. Its outer walls were 70 feet by 50 feet and 15 feet high. The roofs sloped inwards but there were no inner walls. It thus resembled four barns facing inwards to an open space. At each corner was a windowless room, the only fully enclosed spaces.

Their guards were Muslims. The guard commander, Mobit Khan, a villainous looking fellow with a grim sense of humour, began by asking them to regard him as their friend. They were lucky to have such pleasant quarters as its last occupants had been very important people. They had, however, tried to escape, so his Master had been forced to put them to death. He strongly advised them not to make the same mistake. Having eaten nothing all day they asked him for food. He told them he was sorry, but having received no instructions, they would have to wait till the morning.

Next day they were given a fanum, (about 2p), and told that their servants could go to the market to buy things for them. Mobit pointed out that as he had a profound knowledge of local customs it would be to their advantage to give him their money to spend for them. They agreed. But after a few days found themselves with hardly any food and no clothing to keep out the intense night cold.

They protested and Mobit became angry. Did they think that he, a Muslim, would sink to defrauding such miserable creatures? In desperation they appealed to the Kellidar. Mobit indignantly denied their charges. It was they who had asked him to manage their affairs. He had done so only out of the kindness of his heart and was actually out of pocket from giving them all sorts of luxuries. The Kellidar, with admirable diplomacy, scolded them for trying to injure Mobit's reputation but ruled they should be allowed to spend their own money. From then on Mobit did all he could to make their lives miserable. But by almost starving themselves for a month, they managed to save enough to buy some clothing.

On 10th December, twenty seven of the wounded officers left behind at Arni were brought into the prison. The greatly increased numbers spurred on all the inmates to think about organising their lives to make things more comfortable. Each decided to work at a trade. Baird, whenever his wounds allowed, turned his hand to carpentry. Later, with a view to improving their meagre diet, he developed an interest in gardening. The location of the plot where he was allowed to grow vegetables is shown on the plan of the prison. Lindsay took up tailoring and became particularly proud of his shirt making. After their release, Baird carried one of the shirts his friend had made as a talisman wherever he went.

By division of labour and careful saving to buy materials, everyone was provided with a cot, a table, a stool and various articles of clothing. Ways of sharing their handiwork varied from gifts and barter to buying and selling, though anyone too sick to work was given his share.

At daybreak on 10th May 1781 the prisoners' woke to the clatter of chains and saw that several blacksmiths were entering the prison with iron shackles. The Kellidar soon followed escorted by a strong guard and told his captives he had received orders to put them in irons.

Captain Lucas, a Company officer, who had emerged as the prisoners' spokesman, demanded to know why they were to be degraded in this way.*

"Is it your wish," he said "that I, a man with grey hairs who has received thirteen wounds and has been made a cripple for life, should be insulted by being put in irons?"

The Kellidar replied that he must be very ignorant of the way his Master ordered things. Although he was in a position of great power, if he were to fail to carry out his instructions to the letter, to err on the side of leniency or severity, his Master would strip him of all authority.

He then ordered the blacksmiths to do their duty and left telling Mobit to see that the shackling was properly carried out.

When it came to the turn of Baird, whose wounds had re-opened and who was unable to stand, Lucas again intervened, asking indignantly if it was Hyder's intention to put this prisoner to death, for that would be the certain result of shackling Baird in his present state. Mobit replied that a pair of shackles had been sent for each prisoner and all must be used.

"Then let me be shackled with two pairs," said Lucas.

Mobit, who may have noted the Kelidar's remarks about undue severity and feared to put himself in the wrong, said he would ask for the Book of Fate to be opened to discover what lay in store for Baird. This was done and the reply came that his fate was good. He need not be shackled for the time being.

The logic of this is hard to follow. Perhaps the Kellidar did not fancy having to account for a prisoner's death. Certainly, had he been able to see into the future, Baird would have been the last man to receive mercy.

*A fluent linguist and of indomitable courage, Lucas did much to keep up the spirits of the prisoners with his charm and wit. He was 'highly honoured' by the natives for his skill at chess. A few days before the prisoners were shackled, the Kellidar had to come to the prison for a game with him.

The eight inch chain between the rings on the prisoners' ankles so restricted their movements that they decided to extend their range of sedentary activities. They made playing cards of coarse paper stuck on cloth and boned smooth, and back-gammon tables from strips of bamboo. Swarms of rats had invaded the place so they organised competitions to catch the most in a set time. This pastime had the added advantage of pleasing the guards as they made curries with the carcasses.

Shackling was evidently part of a policy to tighten up security as further restrictions followed. The prisoners were forbidden to buy some articles and the Kellidar came to warn them not to communicate with other prisoners or their ears and noses would be cut off. They were puzzled by all this until they heard that Colonel Baillie had been brought to Seringapatam and was in a house near their prison. That the information came from Baillie himself requires some explanation.

The prisoners had an insatiable desire for news for which they relied on their servants who daily met their counterparts from other prisons in the marketplace. That these men should risk their lives for small gain shows the fascination of intrigue that exists under all despotisms. They would carry a letter in a cake or cheroot, using a pre-arranged form of words to let the other know the contents. British and Sepoy officers, other ranks and sepoys, were all able to communicate and even pass on a little money if the need was desperate.

Towards the end of May, Baird had been carried to the gate of the compound by his friends to observe the people outside. He was watching several white men dressed as Muslims, drilling native soldiers in British fashion when, to his horror, he recognised men from his own company. Catching sight of him they rushed over to the gate weeping bitterly and assuring him that they were acting under duress. Before Baird could reply he was seized by the guard and dragged away.

Some days later he received a letter written by one of the men to Baillie and sent on via the servants. It described how they had been forcibly taken from their comrades, and given a drug called majum, (marijuana), circumcised and initiated into the Muslim faith. After this revelation Baird and his companions had not only the mortification of seeing their men training the enemy but were filled with foreboding lest they should suffer the same fate.

They remained in this state until 10th July when a Brahmin came to ask them if they would enter Hyder's service. They would be richly rewarded and given a greater command than they had held in the British Army. Lucas asked the Brahmin to thank his master and tell him that nothing would induce them to abandon their religion and country. The Brahmin left and did not return. But the prisoners continued to be haunted by thoughts of how completely they were at Hyder's mercy.

By November Baird's wounds had healed over and he was put in irons. Yet the next few months were the least harrowing of their long imprisonment. They were becoming accustomed to the monotony of their days. Even the petty cruelties of Mobit, nicknamed Bruin, had become part of their lives.

He would wake them at dawn and make them stand an hour while the rivets of their irons were minutely inspected. He would call them mutinous rascals if they grumbled and say his Master was too kind to them. He manufactured bad news to depress them. When a twenty one gun was heard he told them the British Army had been defeated and thousands of prisoners would soon be arriving. And, because of their insatiable craving for news, they half believed him.

The sepoy guards, who were open to bribery, also invented news that would vary according to amounts tendered. One day the British were victorious and release was near. The next, Hyder had conquered all the Carnatic. The misery of hearing these accounts exceeded any pleasure. Yet news was a drug and, knowing the information would be false, they continued to question the guards.

Early in 1782 an unexpected event brought them great rejoicing. It began with Mobit insulting a prisoner. Instead of reacting with the usual 'dumb insolence' the prisoner answered back angrily. It was a spark to tinder. The others crowded round Mobit shouting abuse and threats on his life. Thoroughly frightened, Mobit ran out threatening to have their ears and noses cut off.

The Kellidar soon appeared and said Mobit had told him they had beaten him up and were planning to take the fort. The prisoners were now not a little alarmed at their temerity, but Lucas, putting on a bold face said they had endured Mobit's insults long enough and were determined to stand them no longer, even if it meant losing their lives. The Kellidar sternly reprimanded them and left, threatening to have them chained to the floor.

A few days later a guard of Rajputs marched in to take over from Mobit and their old tormentor departed amid shouts and hisses. They never saw him again. A year later they heard, 'with great satisfaction' that he had been killed in a force sent to put down an uprising in the countryside around Seringapatam. Life under their new guards was more pleasant and conditions continued to improve until 20th March.

That day twenty two officers, many wounded and in a filthy state, were brought into the prison. From Colonel Brathwaite's army in Tanjore, they had been attacked and overwhelmed by Tipu's cavalry as they were out in the fields guarding the people harvesting the grain. Tipu had treated them with humanity taking them into his tent and giving them biscuits and money. But once handed over to Hyder they had suffered privation and neglect.

The prison was now terribly overcrowded and although the new batch included a Doctor White, he had no medicine chest. With the monsoon's arrival the inmates were in desperate straits. Their legs swelled up from the chafing of their irons. Some, Baird included, were attacked by dysentery. A sickness like the typhus in English gaols began to spread.

The worst affected had 'bloody fluxes' but no European doctors were allowed to see them. Told they could have native doctors, four accepted. They were given opium which stopped the flow of blood. But within twenty-four hours all four had died. To the horror of the survivors, their corpses were unceremoniously dragged out to feed the jackals. Among them was Captain Lucas who had almost certainly saved Baird's life and had been an inspiration to all. His loss at this low ebb came as a crushing blow.

With the end of the monsoons, conditions began to mend slowly. But the year dragged on in an atmosphere of mounting hopelessness. On 19th November they heard that Colonel Baillie was dead. After his first defiant stance he had been singled out by Hyder for special punishment. He had been presented to the people for abuse and insult. Since leaving Arcot he had been kept in irons in solitary confinement. He had received no medical treatment and it seems certain that Hyder intended his death.

The mood of the dwindling band of prisoners fluctuated with reports of outside events. Early in 1783 their hopes were raised by news of an attack on the Malabar Coast by an army from Bombay under General Matthews. Next they heard that Tipu had marched from the Carnatic and was poised to drive the invaders into the sea. Anxiously waiting for further tidings, they became aware of unmistakeable signs of confusion and fear both inside and outside the prison. When questioned the guards refused to explain, saying it would be more than their lives were worth.

At last, after solemn promises of secrecy, they were told that Hyder Ali was dead. For prisoners and guards the news seemed world shattering. But while the guards looked to the future with foreboding, the

TIPU SULTAN

prisoner's feelings were of intense relief. They compared Hyder's severity with the kindness shown by his son, Tipu. Surely their lot must now take a turn for the better.

The first sign of change came with the arrival of a new Kellidar who immediately clapped the old one in prison and replaced the Rajput guards with Muslims. This was a matter for regret, and yet, the prisoners argued, changes were only to be expected. A new ruler was bound to place men he could trust in key positions. And, as events soon showed, Tipu was vulnerable to treachery.

On hearing of his father's death, he had left the Malabar Coast for the Carnatic to establish his authority over his main army. A few days later, the Kellidar of Bednore had surrendered the fort with its treasures to the Bombay army. Assured of his army's loyalty, Tipu hurried again across his kingdom to avenge the loss.

To the prisoners, anxiously waiting to hear the fate of the British at Bednore came conflicting rumours. Then on 5th June they heard that Tipu had recaptured the fort and taken many prisoners including General Matthews. At the same time came orders for their rations to be cut and for their servants no longer to shop for them in the bazaar. They would have to rely on the guards for all necessities.

On 20th June they saw General Matthews arrive in a palanquin, dressed in uniform and surrounded by his servants but under a strong guard. A few days later they heard he had been shackled in solitary confinement.

Soon after came a rumour that Tipu had laid siege to Mangalore, a strongly fortified town on the Malabar Coast held by a British garrison under Colonel Campell. It seemed just one more event that would rack their nerves until the inevitable day when the guards would tell them the place had been taken. But, as the weeks passed with no news of its fall, they heard that the task was more difficult than Tipu had expected.

At the end of September the last shreds of faith in the humanity of their new master were torn away. They heard that General Matthews had been poisoned. From now on, only the most sanguine believed they could survive and even they realised that their lives hung by a single thread - the defence of Mangalore where Tipu had committed so large a part of his army that its capture had become a matter of honour.

On 20th November an unusual event aroused in the prisoners a mixture of surprise, pleasure and resentment. A purse containing 13 pagodas was smuggled to Captain Judson, one of the officers captured at Tanjore with Colonel Brathwaite's army. It had been carried all the way from Madras by the mother of a sepoy, captured at the same time. Believing her son to be still alive, she had told Judson's wife of her intention to travel to Mysore, calling at all the places where prisoners were held until she found him. Mrs Judson gave the woman 13 pagodas, asking her to deliver them to her husband if she found where he was.

Wandering from place to place for more than a year, the woman reached Seringapatam, where, at a communal well, the usual place for gossip, she got word of her son and of Judson. That the woman had made the journey through a foreign country in safety seemed remarkable. Even more so was the honesty of the poor people through whose hands the money had passed. But the fact that a simple woman had been able to accomplish so much on her own, not only filled the prisoners with admiration, it fired their resentment against the Madras Government. For, with all the resources at its disposal, no attempt had been made to contact them. As one prisoner wrote ironically:

"The attention of the Government could not, of course be expected to equal the cares of maternal affection."*

In the months that followed, nothing occurred to lessen their resentment. Many times they were told by the guards that orders for their assassination had arrived only to be countermanded as the tide of war turned against Tipu. They also heard that he had received emissaries to discuss peace terms. But this they no longer dared believe.

The morning of 2nd March 1784 began like any other with the arrival of the guard commander and the Brahmin who paid them their allowances. Then the names of Baird, Lindsay and Monteith were called out. The three stood up and, to their amazement, were told their irons were to be knocked off and they would be taken from the prison to see the Kellidar.

Their minds were plunged into a turmoil of uncertainty at the thought of leaving the scene of their long years of suffering which, through familiarity, and comradeship had become a refuge in a hostile world. Baird demanded to know the reason for their removal before he would set foot outside the prison. Lindsay said that if he was to die, it would be in the company of his friends and on the spot where they had suffered together.

The Brahmin assured them they would hear nothing but good news. Then, seeing they remained unconvinced, he smiled and said:

*The sepoy's mother remained at Seringapatam and was reunited with her son on his release.

"You have suffered enough. I come to impart joy to you all. The merciful Nabob, my Master, Tipu Sultan, has restored peace to the world. The English Nation and he are now friends. You are immediately to be taken out of irons and tomorrow will leave Seringapatam and march to your own country."

Lindsay remained convinced that treachery was intended until a letter from an army friend containing money for his use was brought to him. For Baird, the vivid memory of that moment of freedom was never dimmed. In after years when recalling it his eyes would light up as though experiencing again the intense relief and excitement.

The three had their irons removed and hobbled out of prison with the tiny eight inch steps that had become second nature. They were led to the Cutchery (Court House) where a crowd had assembled. Among them were some of the Highlanders who had been forced into Hyder's service. They fell on their knees and pleaded with Baird to intercede for them. He consoled them and promised to do his best to get their release. Inside the Cutchery the Kellidar smilingly confirmed that the war was over and all prisoners would be set free.

"I take it then," said Baird, "that all the British will be allowed to leave."

"Not so much as a dog shall be left behind," said the Kellidar.

"Then I claim these," Baird said, laying his hands on two of the young soldiers. But the Kellidar gave a sign to the guard who surrounded the men and hustled them away.

The three officers were taken to Colonel Brathwaite, who had been in separate confinement, and were given the first letters from home and friends since their capture. Baird also received money from the officers of the 73rd for himself and other survivors.

The following day, at a village a few miles from the fort, they were joined by all the other prisoners including the small number of men from their regiment who were still alive. They had, too, the satisfaction of rewarding those guards who had shown them kindness.

The British other ranks had been treated in much the same way as their officers, for Hyder's only concern had been for safe custody and economy, with little regard for rank. Their death rate had been higher because they lacked the training and ability of the officers to organise their lives.

The Highlanders suffered most, due, it was said, to homesickness and the constraints of prison life after the freedom of their native hills and glens. Of the 110 captured only 30 came out alive and few of these saw active service again. The sepoys had been forced into hard labour and brutally treated. But the harshest treatment was meted out to the native officers, who Hyder regarded as traitors. They bore their suffering with fortitude and few deserted to the enemy.

The prisoners continued to harbour resentment against the Madras Government for making no attempt to contact them and were grateful only to Warren Hastings, the Governor General at Calcutta, who raised the money to wage war against Hyder; to General Sir Eyre Coote who led the Madras Army; and to Captain Dallas who made strenuous efforts with his cavalry escort to organise their safe return from the prisons in Mysore.

Lord Macartney, Governor of Madras, had mismanaged the peace settlement. He had ordered an army of 15,000 men, advancing from the south and well on its way to Seringapatam, to withdraw, knowing full well that Tipu was ignoring the armistice and continuing the siege of Mangalore. Mangalore fell and Tipu was able to dictate terms to the three frightened commissioners who had been sent into Mysore with Dallas' small cavalry escort. He agreed to release the British prisoners but, in practice, they remained at his mercy. In the last resort their lives depended on the ceaseless energy and courage of Captain Dallas. More than 300 prisoners who had been forced into the Muslim faith and were regarded by Tipu as having renounced their British allegiance were never released or seen again. Nor were these the last casualties of the Madras Government's haste to end hostilities. From the seeds of their ineptitude were to grow two more devastating wars in which David Baird would play increasingly important roles.

CHAPTER 4

Release, promotion, first return to Seringapatam. 1784-1791

Baird had never wavered in his belief that he would be released and had done what he could to prepare for it. Within the limits of wounds, confinement and shackling, he had tried to keep in shape with carpentry, gardening and other activities.

After Dr. White arrived he had many conversations with him on hygiene, diet and the prevention of disease, particularly as they affected the health of the soldier. From these discussions he acquired information which he used later to maintain the health of those under his command.

The mistakes made by their leaders in the campaign leading to their imprisonment - the lack of preparation, the indecision and errors of judgement and the difficulties involved in the attempt to unite two wings of an army - were endlessly discussed. The conclusions drawn would exercise Baird's mind in years to come, when his reactions are seen to be influenced by his first traumatic experience of battle.

Of his rehabilitation we know little except that on his release his large frame was skeletal, his wounds had still not healed, his body had broken out in sores and the ball was at last removed from his leg. We also know that he was abstemious in his habits and actively sought physical fitness. He said that his greatest privation had been lack of food and there had been times when he had to restrain himself from snatching food out of the hands of other prisoners.

Through the years of suffering and death in the prison community composed of many different nationalities and characters, there can be few facets of courage and frailty he had not witnessed. He apparently succeeded in putting the past out of mind, for he rarely spoke of his ordeal and when he did, tended to play it down. Perhaps because of this suppression and the demands of his profession, he appears as a dual personality: the hard-headed soldier, imposing rigid discipline, and the warm hearted friend, sensitive to the sufferings of others and liable to unexpected displays of emotion.

He found his Regiment seething with discontent on the thorny subject of promotion. Before leaving for home, the G. O. C., General Stuart, had recommended Lord William Murray, a junior half-pay captain for the majority that had fallen vacant. The other officers, regarding this as an injustice to Baird, their senior captain, had sent off a memorial protesting to the Horse Guards.

The reply which came months later refused to confirm Murray's appointment and found Baird the proper choice. But as the Second Battalion had just been disbanded, Colonel George MacKenzie, with other officers, would soon be joining them so there was no vacancy to fill. Although in a position to purchase promotion in another regiment with his accumulated back pay from the years in prison, Baird was content to take his chance and wait.

In the event he waited three years, when a chain of promotion was created by the sudden death of Colonel MacKenzie and he was able to purchase his majority. Soon after the move he was himself struck down by the only illness, apart from wounds, of his long service in India. His recovery owed little to medical attention and a great deal to the kindness of a Scottish couple who took him into their home and nursed him back to health.

The following year, after an absence of a decade, he sailed home on leave. He found many changes. His mother had not long died. The family business was flourishing in Scotland's growing prosperity. His eldest brother, Robert, was again in residence at Newbyth, his country seat and was hoping to enter Parliament through his friendship with Henry Dundas, who controlled the notoriously undemocratic Scottish electoral system for the Tories. Most of his sisters had married men of substance. Charlotte, the youngest, said to be very beautiful, was the wife of Lord Haddo, heir to the Earl of Aberdeen and, incidentally, the mother of the Prime Minister at the time of the Crimean War.

So, with a lull in warlike activities in Europe, Baird gave himself up to the pleasures of life with family, friends and the field sports in which he excelled.

This pleasant existence lasted almost three years and did much to rehabilitate him in mind and body. It was suddenly interrupted by a letter from India which began:

"Before you read another line, order post horses for an immediate dash to the Horse Guards."

The writer, Captain Dalrymple, senior captain of Baird's regiment, (now renumbered 71st Foot), went on to explain that their C.O. had been put on a ship for England and was so ill he was not expected to last the voyage. Baird must lose no time if he wanted the command - and would he, at the same time, secure the majority for the writer?

Baird arrived in London to find his C.O's. death had been notified to the Horse Guards and the vacancy filled by an officer whose sole aim was to acquire the command of a regiment, with no desire to serve in India. This individual told Baird he would be happy to let him have the 71st if he could find another lieutenant-colonel willing to sell out, paid him for his rank and saw to it the commissions and exchanges were gazetted on the same day.

Baird eventually tracked down an officer willing to take part in the transaction and was about to conclude the deal when he discovered that his agent in Scotland had failed to send on the money. Unable to account for the delay, he retired with a friend into a coffee house to talk the matter over. He had just walked out when he was overtaken by a fellow Scot who had sailed home with him from India. The man confessed to overhearing the conversation and offered to advance the money. Baird thanked him but said he would have to decline the offer as he could not be sure the delay was not due to a more sinister cause than negligence on the part of his agent.

The money arrived on 8th December and Baird became C.O. of the 71st. But because of the delay and his delicacy in not accepting the loan, Sir John Moore and Lord Cavan were both gazetted above him. He would meet both these officers on active service and serve under them and it is curious how the course of history was altered by this trifling event.*

Baird returned to Madras in 1791 to find his Regiment on active service with Lord Cornwallis, Governor General and C-in-C the Army, against the old enemy, Tipu Sultan, in the third campaign of the War. The first, led by Major-General Medows, had ended in disastrous defeat. The second, under Cornwallis, would have succeeded had not the monsoons and widespread sickness forced him to destroy his siege train and return to Madras in May 1790.

Appointed to command a brigade of sepoys, Baird took part in capturing the numerous hill forts in order to secure communications as the army advanced. On 5th February, they arrived at a position to the north of Seringapatam, under the French Rocks with the Locani River to the left and a large tank to the right. From this vantage point the great fortified town was viewed with curiosity by the whole army. But for Baird the feelings roused were far deeper. Memories came flooding back and for a while he found it impossible to control his emotions. At length they were replaced by grim satisfaction that against all the odds he had returned to the contest with his gaoler on more equal terms.

*It is also remarkable that at the time Baird was involved in this transaction, Sir John Moore was in Ireland trying to obtain the command of the 51st Foot and was also anxious about the late arrival of his purchase money. But, unlike Baird, when it turned up his promotion was backdated to 30th November.

Since he had left the place seven years ago, Tipu had greatly reinforced its defences which now comprised three separate lines. A bound hedge of bamboo enclosed areas to the north and south of the River. To the north it extended almost the length of the Island, varying in depth from a mile on the west side to half a mile on the east. On the west side, several redoubts had been constructed while beyond the Locani River, the Carrigaut Hills were fortified to command the ford across the Cauvery.

Should the defenders be forced to retreat over the Cauvery they could take up prepared positions in the Pettah (village) in the centre and in the Lal Bagh (Palace Gardens) in the eastern corner of the Island, where batteries also commanded the river crossing. The third line was the immensely strong citadel containing Tipu's Palace and the prison where Baird had been held.

Because of the approaching monsoon season Cornwallis decided not to wait for an army from Bombay led by General Sir Robert Abercromby on its way from the west, but to mount an attack at once. It was to be three pronged, with divisions led by General Medows, himself and Colonel Maxwell. Baird was Maxwell's second-in-command and would lead the division into action.

On 6th February he went with Maxwell to reconnoitre the enemy's right while Medows and his a-d-c, Colonel George Harris (of whom much will be heard later), performed a similar operation on the left. After receiving their reports Cornwallis issued orders for the attack which began simply:

"The army marches in three divisions at 7 in the evening to attack the enemy's camp and lines."

The advance was to be in parallel lines with the outside divisions turning Tipu's flanks and joining up with the centre.

That Cornwallis should tempt providence by a night attack is surprising, as he had only by good fortune escaped disaster in a night march in his previous campaign. The only advantage of the plan seems to have been that of surprise on which he must have been relying.

The assault began with the three divisions at once plunged into the hazards to be expected from masses of men operating in the dark, in unknown territory and against an unseen enemy.

Baird's first objective was the defence post on Carrigaut Hill. About a mile from the bound hedge he came upon the enemy's advance guard and, at the same time, spotted a detachment of cavalry escorting a party of rocket men sent to harass the British camp. The cavalry beat a rapid retreat, leaving the rocket men to do what they could to delay the British advance.

The hillside was instantly lit up with musket fire, wildly directed at invisible targets. The redoubt had meanwhile been identified and Baird led a dash at it, mounting the earthwork and scattering the defenders with the bayonet. Keeping up his momentum, he charged another post where the enemy had regrouped. After slight resistance they too fled and the hill was taken.

He had halted for Maxwell to arrive and together they tried to gauge the progress of the second division by observing the line of fire. It appeared to be gaining ground, so Maxwell told Baird to proceed down the hill towards the bound hedge and pointed out the road to take. Ordering his men to follow, Baird made off at a run, only to find the road petering out into a rocky, steeply winding track that ended at a stream. He paused and, turning round, was amazed to find only one officer and about a dozen soldiers. He then heard firing on the left and setting off in that direction came upon the main body of his men, who had taken a longer but less precipitous descent.

Without delay he continued the pursuit of the Mysoreans across the Locani, through the bound hedge and into the enemy camp, all in the face of fire from the far side of the Cauvery and from Tipu's forces on the right. Soon after he joined up with Cornwallis' division, though not before disaster had been narrowly averted when the 71st and 72nd were about to fire on each other.

Baird now decided to attempt a crossing of the Cauvery, which was known to be fordable in places at this time of year.

Under fire from both sides of the river he set off with a party of Highlanders at what appeared to be a suitable spot. Through water up to the shoulder they made it to the island and, with ammunition soaked, Baird ordered a careful advance into the darkness with bayonets at the ready. Within minutes they came upon a battery and were about to charge when they realised that it was in the hands of their comrades. They were joined soon after by Maxwell and this proved the end of hostilities.

By a mixture of courage, impetuosity and luck, Cornwallis' gamble had paid off. The centre and left columns had met at the appointed place while Tipu had withdrawn most of his army into the old City, though only by the skin of his teeth. As the gates were closing he had narrowly escaped capture by one of his ex-prisoners, John Lindsay.

Two divisions had been accounted for, but what of the third? Having been delayed by attacking a redoubt he had been specifically told to bypass, Medows had suffered several severe casualties. He had then attempted to discover Cornwallis' whereabouts by retreating behind the bound hedge, lost his way and ended up on Carrigaut Hill. A sensitive man who generally managed to hide his anxiety with a show of flippancy, Medows was extremely mortified at his failure.

The army now settled down to wait for Abercromby's reinforcements while Tipu put up some ineffective resistance. On 24th he capitulated and signed a treaty ceding half his territories to the East India Company, together with a huge indemnity of 33,000,000 rupees. He also agreed to exchange all prisoners and hand over two of his sons as hostages.

At the time of the handing over ceremony, Medows, still depressed by his mistakes, was in his tent attempting to commit suicide by firing a bullet into his side. The bullet dropped out of the cartridge though the wadding entered his body, causing an ugly wound. It was later suggested that his attempt was less than determined. Had he meant to kill himself he would have blown out his brains.

The army was disappointed at not being allowed to storm the Citadel, but was awarded prize money by the East India Company. Cornwallis and Medows distributed their share, £44,000 and £14,000 respectively, to the troops. Baird, as lieutenant-colonel, received £968, which he kept.

CHAPTER 5

Tanjore

After the Peace Treaty, Baird spent his time at Secundamalli, improving the efficiency and discipline of his Regiment. He was at the surrender of Pondicherry and in July 1793 was posted as Commandant of the small state of Tanjore, some 170 miles to the south west of Madras. The appointment was partly a civil one as, a few years previously, the Commandant had been instructed, for economy reasons, to take over the functions of Civil Resident. Sir Charles Oakley, the Madras Governor, had known Baird since he first arrived in India and probably regarded Tanjore as an appropriate initiation to civil administration for his protege.

But as so often in Indian politics, the situation in that tiny State was more complex than appeared. Protected by the British Army and with its destiny controlled by Madras, it was, as Macaulay wrote of such states, 'at the mercy of any ruler of great talents and few scruples'.

The succession had for many years been unstable. On the death of the previous Rajah in 1787, a choice had to be made between his brother, Amir Singh and his adopted son, a young boy named Serfogi. Adoption in India conferred all the rights of legitimacy and the late Rajah had named Serfogi as his heir. He had even begged the German missionary, Friedrich Schwartz, an old man but powerful in Indian politics, to become guardian of the boy's welfare.

To assess the claims, Madras called in Native legal experts. Not surprisingly, their choice of Amir Singh suited their masters. Serfogi could not have assumed power for years and would have become the focus of internal intrigue. However, keeping their options open, Madras agreed that, though irregular, adoption was not illegal. Amir Singh was thus placed on trial. Should he prove uncooperative, Serfogi's claims could be re-examined.

Events now followed a familiar route on the march to British ascendency in India. Dissension arose between Tanjore and Madras over supplies for the war against Tipu. About the same time Schwartz discovered that the Rajah was trying to eliminate his rival, Serfogi, by the oriental device of confining him in a darkened room and denying him all education. A few months later, ostensibly to allay Schwartz' fears for the boy's safety, he was returned to Madras. This served to increase pressure on the Rajah to pay revenues that were falling into arrears.

Raising money was the crux of the Rajah's problems. Potentially prosperous, Tanjore's ancient farming and tax gathering systems were quite incapable of meeting the ever increasing demands of Madras. To make matters worse, Shiverow, the Rajah's chief minister, was feathering his own nest at the State's expense. Too weak and incompetent to initiate change or control the depredations of his minister, the Rajah was caught in a trap from which there was no escape.

All communications between Madras and the Rajah passed through Baird's office so that he was well briefed on the situation. At first the Rajah had resented the procedure as a slight to his status as an independent ruler and Oakley had instructed Baird to visit the Palace, pay the Rajah every attention and comply with his wishes wherever possible. Suspicious at first, the Rajah was won over by Baird's sincerity and soon began treating him as a friend and confidant. Inevitably, Baird's sympathies were aroused.

As the Madras Government's representative on the spot, self-interest should have urged caution in this web of intrigue. But, a tyro in the game, he continued to act on the principles that had so far guided him in his career, which for the niceties of diplomacy could hardly have been worse adapted. Altruism at any time would have been unwise: events that now begin to unfold were to make it a downright folly.

In September 1795, Oakley sailed for England and was replaced by one determined to carve a name for himself in British Colonial history. Lord Hobart was born in 1760 and began his career as a soldier. Entering politics in 1787, he distinguished himself by outright opposition to the political concessions to Roman Catholics by Pitt and Dundas. He was appointed to Madras with the promise of the Governor-Generalship to follow.

As the means of achieving his ambition, he now decided to extend British rule over the Native States. This, as he well knew, ran counter to the official policy laid down by the Company's Directors in London, which was to expand trade, increase profits and leave the Native Rulers to their own devices. He must also have known that he could expect no support from the Governor-General at Calcutta as Sir John Shore, an old Company servant, had been specifically chosen to carry out the policy of the Directors. But to Lord Hobart there was a factor that was even more calculated to fuel his resentment at any opposition from that quarter. Sir John was his social inferior. That he, an aristocrat, should be thwarted in his designs by a jumped-up Company writer, rankled from the start.

The feuding began in his first year of office. The Nabob of Carnatic was heavily in debt to the Company. Without reference to Shore, Hobart threatened to seize the district of Tinnevelly as payment. Shore pointed out that this was an infringement of the Nabob's rights and when Hobart insisted he appealed to London.

While a decision was awaited, Hobart turned his attention to Tanjore. It was small but rich. It was firmly under British control but was inefficiently governed and failing to pay for the protection it was getting. He was unlikely to see Baird, a King's officer, as the man to carry out the changes he had in mind. He had also caught wind of Baird's friendship with the Rajah, which, if allowed to continue, could impede his plans.

Baird's first intimation of Hobart's intentions came in September 1794. The flow of official letters to the Rajah through his office came to a halt. On enquiries he found that the Rajah was receiving them by ordinary post. Realising that he had been acting solely on the precedent of his predecessor with no official mandate, he wrote to Madras on 3rd October asking to be confirmed in the civil appointment. His request was refused.

In November the post of Civil Resident was revived in the person of Alexander McLeod, a Company servant whose arrival must have been unpalatable to Baird. But the events it precipitated require deeper explanation than pique.

Between the King's officers and the Company servants there existed a natural suspicion. Each was moved by self-interest and, with differing aims and loyalties, there was always the sense that aggrandisement of one could only be at the expense of the other. With Baird and McLeod, these antipathies were exacerbated by wide character differences. McLeod evidently delighted in intrigue and subterfuge with the power it gave others. Baird was at the opposite pole. His dislike of double dealing was evident to all who knew him. "No man durst avow an evil intention to his face," wrote an officer who served with him for many years.*

Normally he would have left McLeod to his devices. But he was already involved and seemingly unable to extricate himself with honour. At the heart of the matter was the character and plight of the Rajah. No better or worse than the average petty potentate of his time, Amir Singh, before the arrival of the British, would have ruled as a despot, fallen to the internal plotting of a rival or become the satrap of a stronger neighbour. His position was now different, though hardly less invidious. He was restrained from exercising the extreme ruthlessness that would have secured his throne, yet he was subject

*General Middlemore.

to the intrigues of his ministers. The British grip, though gentler, was as relentless as his predecessors had endured under powerful neighbours.

McLeod's instructions were to keep a watchful eye on the Rajah and his ministers, in order to avert "those evils which there is much reason to apprehend will fall upon the Tanjore country in consequence of the dissipation and extravagance which had marked the conduct of His Excellency and the Persons in authority under him".

He began by investigating the Palace administration.

The Rajah, thoroughly alarmed, confided his fears to Baird. McLeod was not only disrespectful to him, a ruling monarch, but was unjust in his criticism of how he was running his affairs. He had accused him of appointing Shiverow, 'a corrupt person', as his chief minister and of not establishing an open court. These were matters that did not break his Treaty with the British. He was responsible for his servant and dispensed justice to his people in the time-honoured way. His position on the throne was guaranteed by the Treaty so long as he paid his revenues, and this he was ready to do.

McLeod had told him that the Treaty was out of date and unless he signed a new one, handing over the revenues of his country for the next five years, he would meet the fate of the Ruler of Trichinopoly who had been imprisoned and his territories annexed. All this, said the Rajah, was intended to frighten him into signing a new treaty which would mean his being pensioned off and his country handed over to the Company.

Proof that his fears were justified came on the evening of 28th December when Baird received a letter from McLeod requesting him to send a company of men immediately to the street outside the Palace gate and to wait there for instructions. The troops duly arrived and waited as ordered. After a few minutes the officer in charge was handed a note from inside the Palace, signed by McLeod, informing him that his presence was no longer required.

At this obvious act of intimidation, Baird wrote to McLeod drawing his attention to a Government Order defining the limits of military and civil powers. He could not, he said, comply with any future requests for troops unless he was informed of the purpose for which they were required. This was necessary so that he could decide on the size of the force necessary for its execution.

His protest was reasonable and it would have been well had he left it there, but his concern for the Rajah leading him beyond the bounds of prudence, he despatched copies of the correspondence with McLeod to Hobart and to his immediate superior, Colonel Floyd.

From Hobart he naturally received no satisfaction. The orders he quoted did not apply to the present circumstances. He must supply any armed force requested by the Civil Resident.

Floyd, whose sympathies were with Baird, wrote at greater length. He had got in touch with McLeod who told him he had orders to execute some object of a secret nature which meant it was essential to have a considerable force at his disposal. Floyd therefore advised Baird that, as McLeod was acting in the name of the Governor, he would have to do as he was told.

Neither of these replies reached Baird directly but were sent to McLeod with instructions to divulge them when he thought necessary.

Armed with support from both civil and military authorities, McLeod acted promptly. On 23rd January he sent Baird three letters. The first gave instructions that neither Shiverow, the Rajah's chief minister, nor his brothers were to leave the Palace. In the second he said that he had had an official letter regarding the use of troops which he would probably send the same day. The third he sent at 6 in the evening, enclosing the letter from Floyd and requiring Baird to send as large a part of the Garrison, both European and Sepoy, as could be spared to parade in front of his (McLeod's) house, with orders to the officer in command to carry out any instructions that would be given.

Convinced that physical force was about to be used against the Rajah, Baird sent a message to McLeod begging him to explain the purpose of so large a force. Receiving a curt refusal, he waited until the appointed time, mobilised his men then went to see McLeod who was in the house of Schwartz. He asked again that the troops should not be used. If McLeod would let him go with him into the Palace, he would guarantee that the Rajah would comply with any demands made by the Government. His Country's honour, he said, would be better served by this means than by subjecting a ruling monarch to threats of violence by marching troops against him.

McLeod remaining adamant, Baird sent orders for the troops to be posted between the Resident's house and the Palace. He then placed himself at the head of the troops to see that the orders were carried out and to ensure the personal safety of the Rajah. After waiting several hours in the street, he was handed a note from McLeod informing him the force was no longer required and could be dismissed.

Next morning, unaware of what had transpired in the Palace, he sent off his latest correspondence with McLeod to Hobart, together with an account of his own actions during the parading of the troops.

A day later the Rajah, in great distress, informed him that he had been coerced into signing a treaty handing over three of his districts to the East India Company. McLeod had reminded him that Serfogi was still in Madras and that Shiverow would be arrested as soon as he set foot outside the Palace. Yet as soon as the treaty was signed, McLeod had smilingly told him that he could keep Shiverow as his chief minister as a reward for his cooperation. He had signed the treaty only because of threats and from fear of what might happen when the troops were being paraded outside his Palace. But now he had time to reflect he had decided to appeal to the Madras and Calcutta Governments for the restoration of his territories.

Up to this point Baird had been unwise but had committed no irretrievable act of folly. Now, with understandable concern for his friend's predicament and an incredible lack of concern for his own interests, he supported the Rajah's appeal by sending copies of the correspondence he had on the subject to Sir John Shore.

That his intervention had no effect on the outcome is certain. The affair had become a personal contest between Shore and Hobart, who decided on the Rajah's appeal with all the expected casuistry.

According to Hobart, Tanjore was being ruined by the present administration and must be taken over by the Company to bring prosperity and justice to its people. The Rajah's signature had not been obtained by force. He was under the thumb of his chief minister Shiverow, who had taken refuge in the Palace where he could not be arrested. The show of force was intended to show him (Shiverow) that his power was at an end. It was certainly not to force the Rajah into signing the treaty. The truth was he had been only too glad to sign to get rid of the minister.

Shore on the other hand, decided that the Rajah had not signed the treaty willingly and 'with great pleasure' as was suggested. This was proved by the absence of correspondence to show that any negotiations leading to the settlement had taken place, that troops had been paraded outside the Palace when McLeod was with the Rajah and by the use of Mr Schwartz, who had always been opposed to Amir Singh. Finally, as the proper revenues had been paid, there were no grounds for taking over the administration of the State. For all these reasons the Madras Government must hand back the Rajah's territories.*

For the Rajah this was a famous victory and for Baird a victory of sorts. But the frustration of Hobart and McLeod is easily imagined

*For Hobart this humiliation was the last straw. His letters of vituperation against Shore to the India Board became so paranoic that Henry Dundas, head of the board, gave up reading them.

and, not surprisingly, they used every device to delay the restoration. The last occurred on 2nd September 1796, when the handing back ceremony was to take place.

To mark the occasion, the Rajah had asked Baird to fire a Royal Salute, as 'all his nobles and principal men would be there to offer their congratulations'. Baird, who had not been invited to the ceremony, gave his consent ordering the NCO in charge to take his instructions from the Rajah.

By 2.30 pm, having heard no Salute, Baird sent a messenger to find the reason. The man returned to say that, on hearing a Salute was to be fired, McLeod had told the Rajah that the Country could not be handed over until he had consulted Hobart on the matter. Baird then sent orders for the men to leave the battery. But soon after he heard the sound of firing and assumed that McLeod had changed his mind and the handing over had taken place.

Next morning he was surprised to find this had not been done. The Rajah, rather than admit to having been deceived in the eyes of his people, had called back the firing party and told them to fire the Salute. On hearing this Baird wrote immediately to Hobart giving his account of what had occurred.

Four days later he received a letter from Madras informing him that orders had been sent to Floyd (now a major-general) for the immediate removal of the 71st Regiment to Pondicherry. The reason for the move was not given and Baird, officially at least, assumed it was because of an emergency. Informing Madras that his Regiment was 'as always ready to march at an hour's notice', he asked if he was to proceed by forced marches. Receiving no reply he arrived at Trichinopoly a few days later to find orders directing him to change his route to Wallajabad.

Without making it explicit, the Government had got rid of him. Nor was he left in doubt as to Hobart's feelings. In a letter of 14th September, he was told that his orders to fire a salute to mark the restoration of the Rajah's territories were 'unnecessary and improper' and that, by acting on messages from the Palace, he had opposed the order that forbade all Europeans to communicate with the Rajah except through the Resident. As, however, he had been recalled from Tanjore, the President would refrain from further animadversions on his conduct.

This reprimand reached Baird after an unaccountable delay of two months. His reply closed his disastrous entry into public life, the echoes of which would haunt him for many years to come.

He was sorry that Lord Hobart had formed the opinion that he had opposed the orders of the Government. By sanctioning a Salute he thought he had shown a proper respect, not only for the Rajah, but for the Government that was ordering the restoration. The Resident had never before objected when he had fired Salutes and granted guards at the request of the Rajah.

As to being recalled from Tanjore, he begged to say that he had not been recalled but ordered to march with his Regiment. He had since learnt that the reason was to be on hand to embark for the Cape and, if necessary, form an army in the field.

Being unconscious of deserving the animadversions of the President, he was sorry that any part of his conduct should have been misconstrued into the slightest disrespect for the Government.

At the out-station of Wallajabad he had a year to reflect on the course he had taken at Tanjore. He had lost a lucrative appointment, made an enemy of the most powerful man in the Presidency and earned a reputation for setting himself up against authority. Nor could he have failed to realise that all this had taken place because of his attempt to apply his private morality to the pragmatic world of politics. Whether he would learn from his mistakes, only time would show.

Meanwhile he turned his energies to perfecting the discipline and efficiency of his Regiment. In January 1797 it was inspected by Sir Alured Clarke, the C-in-C, who was so impressed that he advised all officers arriving in Madras to break their journey at Wallajabad to observe how best to maintain discipline and arrange the interior economy of their regiments while in India.

From Clarke's General Order and various first hand accounts, Baird was evidently putting into practice the lessons learnt at Lochie's Academy. Nowhere is this more apparent than in the demands he was making on his officers. On five days a week they were on parade at sunrise, taking part with the men in all the drill and manoeuvres. On Sunday morning, he inspected the barrack rooms with the company officers waiting to receive him.

Particular care was taken of the men's welfare. Each man regularly received the allowance due to him, a procedure by no means universally adhered to for, in some regiments, the rank and file were regularly short-changed with no means of redress against the conniving officers.

Corporal punishment was rare. Most offenders were given set hours of work in the garden which provided the Regiment with vegetables. The garden was itself an innovation, one of the few good things to result from Baird's imprisonment.

The Regimental Fund was kept in a healthy state. Part was used to support the Regimental School, another unusual feature. Baird and his officers had none of the fear of encouraging literacy in the ranks which still permeated many English regiments even a century later.

Each soldier's wife received a weekly allowance on condition she kept her children clean and tidy. On Sunday, all who appeared 'respectably dressed' were given rewards as encouragement. Paternalistic as these measures now appear, it is hard to imagine how better to improve the lot of those under the care of a commanding officer, in the conditions then prevailing.

In his personal life Baird was temperate. He never needed to stand aloof to establish his authority. This was vouched for by many who served with him at different times. As one later wrote: 'he was the friend and social companion of his officers, joining in their amusements and sharing their happiness.'

In the summer of 1797, an expedition against the Dutch in Manila was projected. The 71st was backed by the C-in-C for its efficiency and readiness to take part. It was overlooked in favour of the 12th and 33rd, the latter newly arrived from England and commanded by Arthur Wellesley, 'an old friend' of Lord Hobart.

Baird expressed his disappointment in a letter to a friend:

'I have often thought of returning to Europe, but, at such a time, how is it possible to absent myself from my post'.

How indeed. The expedition was abandoned because of a more imminent danger. There were signs and rumours that Tipu Sultan was again preparing for war. If that came, Baird was determined to be on the scene and his irritation over the choice of regiments faded, though it would be recalled later as the first time young Arthur Wellesley cast a shadow across his career.

One morning in October of the same year, Baird went into his office as usual to open his mail. The first letters were routine. Then he came to one that struck him numb. It was a curt order to disband his Regiment. The fit men were to be drafted into the 73rd and 74th Regiments. He himself was to proceed in four days to Madras and embark for the U.K. with the colours, the officers, the NCOs, the band and drummers and all those no longer fit for service.

The one redeeming feature was the speed with which he had to act. Immediately assembling the Regiment on the barrack square, he announced that an order affecting everyone present had come from Headquarters. He started to read out the order, but, choking with emotion, handed the paper to his adjutant.

The effect on the men was shattering. Those to be drafted saw the bonds with their friends, their officers and their Regiment all fall away. Groans of dismay began to swell up. Baird raised his hand and silenced them. "My poor fellows - not a word - the order must be obeyed."

Turning to the band he gave the order to strike up a popular recruiting song of the day set to a Scottish air and the men were marched to their quarters.

By the fourth morning after the order had been received, the internal affairs of the 71st were wound up. The fit were drafted to the other regiments. Those destined for home began the March to Madras where they arrived on 14th October. Three days later they boarded an East Indiaman for the Cape.

Before that an Order had been issued by Lieutenant-General George Harris, the ex-aide to General Medows and now C-in-C South India. It spoke highly of the 71st and commended "the alacrity with which Colonel Baird had arranged at short warning everything relative to the drafting."*

*The inhuman drafting of men to other regiments continued up to the end of the 18th Century when it was stopped by the Duke of York. The option of returning home was then introduced.

CHAPTER 6

Cape interlude. 1798.

The year 1797 had seen the Naval Mutiny at the Nore and, as Baird sailed into Table Bay, there were unmistakeable signs that it had spread to the Cape. On the masts of the anchored warships hung yellow flags signalling the gruesome end of the drama - the hanging of its leaders at the yardarm. But insurrection had not been confined to the Navy. The threat of mutiny in the Army was about to produce another twist in Baird's career.

Lord Macartney, whose term of office at Madras during the Mysore War had been marred by quarrels with senior officers, was now Governor at the Cape. He was 60 and though suffering from gout, seems to have mellowed.

Having been well received by his Lordship after his release from prison Baird decided to pay him a courtesy visit at Government House. He was met by an officious young ADC who not only refused him admittance but said the Governor would not see him. The reason for the rebuff is a mystery. The man could just have been showing his authority or may have seen reports of Baird's involvement in the Tanjore affair and was anticipating the Governor's wishes. If so, his intuition led him astray. A few hours later Baird received a letter, written by the same ADC, expressing Macartney's regret at not having seen him and begging him to call the next morning.

Baird naturally complied and was greeted cordially by Macartney who went on to make him a surprising proposition. Would he allow the remnants of his Regiment to sail on to England while he remained at the Cape with the rank of brigadier-general on the staff?

The offer was tempting, yet Baird hesitated. Although he had been only two days at the Cape, he was in little doubt why his services were required. The Commanding Officer of the 86th Regiment was about to be court-martialled for insubordination to Sir Francis Dundas, the C-in-C, and was being openly supported by other senior officers. With discipline disintegrating, Macartney was turning to Baird as the man to restore order.

Normally Baird would have jumped at the chance, but his delicacy about personal relationships made him hesitate. He had known Dundas during his boyhood in Edinburgh, while Macartney's quarrels with military leaders at Madras had been notorious. What, he wondered, was the rapport between them? It was hardly a question he could put to the Governor, yet until he knew the answer he felt unable to accept the offer. He asked for 24 hours to consider and to this Macartney readily agreed.

He found that Dundas had gone into the country and would be away for a few days. But, convinced by his enquiries that the Army's troubles were internal and Macartney's aim was to re-establish discipline, he returned next day to Government House and announced his acceptance.

Macartney, putting on a show of frankness, said he fully understood Baird's caution and assured him there had been no unpleasantness between him and Dundas. Then as proof that all his cards were on the table, he said:

"Had I known as much of military gentlemen when I was in India as I have learned since, we should never have had any differences. I should have put the generals between myself and the army as I have done in the present instance."*

Baird's first duty was to preside over the court-martial of the C.O. of the 86th. That settled, the months that followed were amongst the happiest of his career. His 2,000 strong brigade was made up of the predominantly Irish 86th and the so called Scotch Brigade, mainly Scots who had served with the Dutch and were now embodied in the British Army. The 86th, with the volatile temperament of all Irish regiments, had suffered under a stupid C.O. who had so alienated both officers and men that there had been a complete breakdown in discipline.

Baird immediately set the tone by taking personal control for, unlike most officers of the day, he had no inhibitions about rubbing shoulders with the men. Their first task was to clear 'a perfect wilderness of trees' to make a parade ground. His initial approach was light hearted and, having cajoled the men into a good humour, he joined in to demonstrate how the work should be done.

'By this time', wrote a captain in the 86th, 'the very idea of becoming one of General Baird's regiments roused us to zeal and energy.' While the work was in progress he was constantly present, encouraging and praising the men's effort and even restraining some of the more enthusiastic by pointing out that steady, sustained exertion was more efficient than sudden bursts of energy.†

To the 86th, after their recent experiences, this interest and involvement in their work by a high ranking officer came as a complete reve-

†Macartney wrote of Baird in glowing terms to the Duke of York at the Horse Guards explaining why he was keeping him at the Cape. The Duke was not pleased at the appointment being made without his permission.

*Captain Middlemore.

lation. They were equally surprised and delighted when they had completed the parade ground inside a week and could commence their training in the new Dundas System of Drill.†

While this activity was proceeding, the Cape was a veritable crossroads for VIPs. Among them, in February, was Lord Mornington on his way to the Governor-Generalship of India, assiduously cultivating the aura of omnipotence that would surround him when he burst upon the India scene. Already primed by his brother, Colonel Arthur Wellesley, with information on the Indian States and the characters of the important men he would have to deal with, he was intercepting despatches from India and questioning the officers who carried them.

He interviewed Baird and seemed particularly interested in Tanjore. Having told all he knew, Baird gathered that Mornington had definite instructions regarding the State's future. But when he tried to discover what they were, he was told they were known only to Mornington and the Secret Committee of the Company. As Baird suspected, this did not augur well for the Rajah.**

On 10th March, Mornington sailed for Calcutta. Baird remained at the Cape until the end of the year, when news came from England of his promotion to major-general, with orders to return to India taking with him the 86th, the Scotch Regiment and some dragoons.

†Sir David Dundas (1735-1820) compiled his system after studying the Prussian Code for Infantry and Cavalry.

**The legal rights of the two candidates for the throne were re-examined and decided in favour of Serfogi. Amir Singh was deposed and pensioned off.

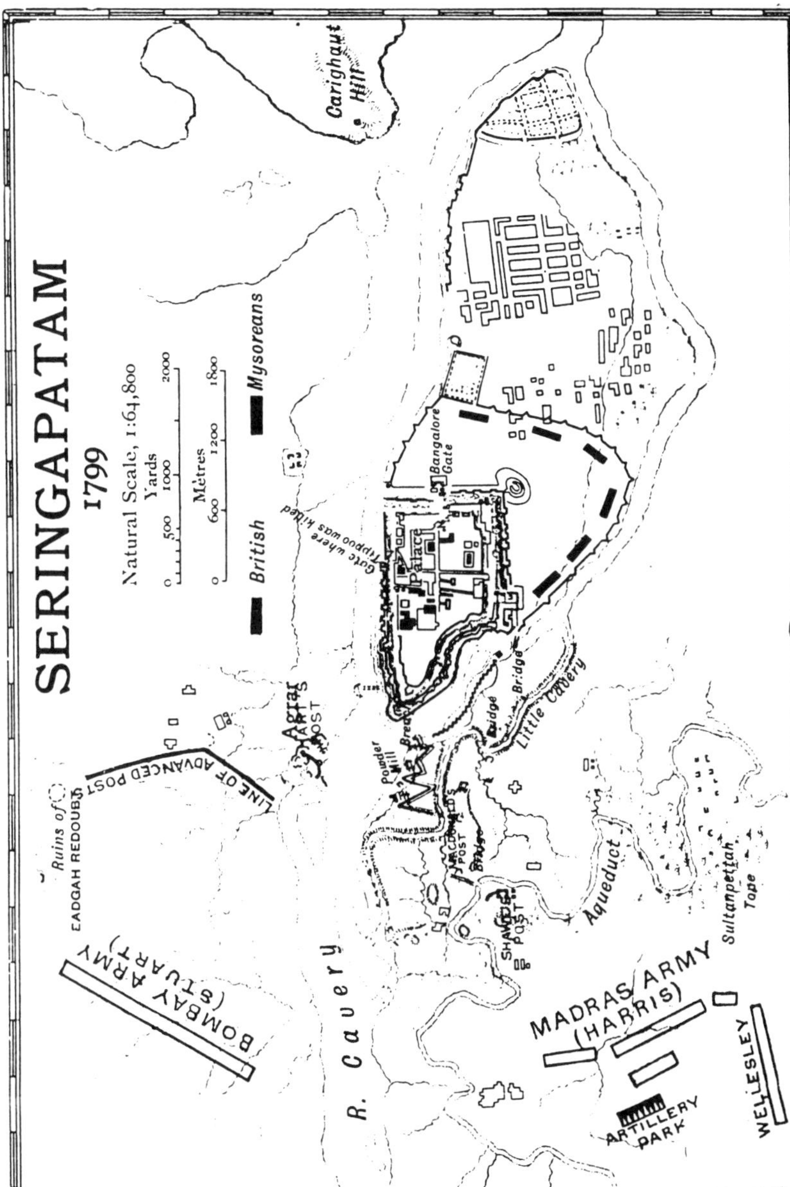
SERINGAPATAM
1799
Natural Scale, 1:64,800
Yards
0 500 1000 2000
Mètres
0 600 1200 1800
British
Mysoreans
Carighaut Hill
Bangalore Gate
Palace
Gate where Tippoo was killed
Agrar ART.S POST
LINE OF ADVANCED POST
Ruins of EADGAH REDOUBT
Powder Mill
Bridge
Little Cavery
Aqueduct
Sultanpettah Tope
R. Cavery
BOMBAY ARMY (STUART)
MADRAS ARMY (HARRIS)
WELLESLEY
ARTILLERY PARK

CHAPTER 7

India. Second return to Seringapatam.

Baird returned to an India of radical change. Lord Mornington had brought to an end the policy of non-involvement in the affairs of Native States and set in motion the British advance to their complete subjugation.

That Mornington should be the instigator of change and one of the chief founders of British India is one of the curiosities of history. For, outside his seven glorious years as Governor-General, there is little to suggest greatness in the man.*

Even his appointment was fortuitous. He was a member of the India Board under the control of Henry Dundas. With Shore approaching retirement, the ever-reliable Cornwallis was asked to take over again as Governor-General while Mornington was offered Madras in place of Hobart. He agreed to this arrangement on condition that, if Cornwallis turned down the offer, he must be Governor-General. Dundas, who had no faith in Mornington's abilities, jibbed at first but was persuaded by Pitt to acquiesce. At the last moment, Cornwallis decided not to go and the senior appointment went to Mornington. By this haphazard concurrence of events, the course of Indian History was changed, as were the lives of many individuals including that of Baird.

Once settled in Calcutta, Mornington's prime objective became the conquest of Mysore and the removal of Tipu Sultan, that perpetual thorn in the British flesh. His reasons were pure expediency, for Tipu had been stripped of much of his power by Cornwallis. He had admittedly intrigued with the French at Mauritius, but, as Mornington well knew, that little episode had all the elements of farce while the only other justification for attacking him, the threat to India posed by Napoleon's army in Egypt, had been removed by Nelson's destruction of the French fleet at the Nile.

Undeterred by these incidents, Mornington was determined to enhance his prestige by some signal victory. In June he ordered the mobilisation of the Madras army, only to learn that it would take many months of preparation before a campaign could be undertaken. Resigned to a long delay, he discovered aspects of the preparation

*For an appraisal of Mornington's character and his fear of able administrators who might oppose his view, see *The Making of the Indian Princes* by Edward Thompson and *Two Views of British India* – The private correspondence of Henry Dundas and Mornington, edited by Edward Ingram.

that roused his concern, not least being the competence of the C-in-C, George Harris and the recently appointed Governor, Lord Clive. Nor was his concern unfounded.

Harris, aide to General Medows in the last Mysore War, had returned to India in 1794 and, having been appointed to the staff at Fort George, had risen to Lieutenant-General and C-in-C in 1796. A brave, kindly, unaffected man, he had no illusions as to his own ability for he attributed his success to good fortune and 'willing privation from self-indulgence'.

As to Lord Clive, he was physically strong though of a rather nervous disposition and his only apparent qualification for high office was being the son of a famous father.

To bring these pawns, for so Mornington regarded them, into the game, he sent his brother Arthur with his Regiment to Madras where the young colonel set about taking control of the campaign preparations. He began by talking Harris into keeping him in Fort George to help steer Lord Clive 'along the right road'. This entailed whole mornings explaining what Mornington meant in his letters, as the information they contained was beyond Clive's comprehension. The strain on young Wellesley must have been considerable, but his efforts were rewarded. He was soon able to inform his brother that Clive was probably not as dull as most people thought and even if he was, not to worry, things were well in hand and he 'would give no trouble'.

In January, Mornington came to Madras to see how things were progressing. He wrote to Dundas at the India Board: 'the improvement of the affairs here, the state of Lord Clive's mind and the advancement of the preparations are to be attributed principally to my brother Colonel Wellesley - - -'.

This then was the set-up into which Baird was about to intrude. After his successful year at the Cape and his promotion to major-general, he was in high hopes that his luck had taken a turn for the better. As a veteran of the Mysore Wars he expected his knowledge of the country and the enemy would be made full use of in the coming campaign. He was in his forty-second year and perhaps over anxious for success. In the hazardous business of soldiering, an opportunity such as now appeared before him was rare and had to be grasped as it might never recur.

Joining the Army at Vellore, he was given command of the first European Brigade, made up of three regiments. This was virtually the same as he had held under Cornwallis when a junior lieutenant-

SIR A. WELLESLEY

MARQUIS WELLESLEY

GENERAL HARRIS

colonel, but as there were three major-generals with the Army, all senior to him, the situation seemed inevitable. Then the Nizam of Hyderabad's army of more than 10,000, led by its native commander, Meer Alum, appeared. Two days later the 33rd was added to it, with the effective command falling on the Regiment's C.O.

That Wellesley, a lieutenant-colonel, should command so large a force roused much comment and Baird tried through unofficial channels to find out the reason. Not satisfied, he wrote to General Harris asking why he, 'a major-general sent expressly by His Majesty to serve on the staff in India, should remain in command of three battalions while a lieutenant-colonel in the same army is placed at the head of seven, or rather thirteen corps - - -'. He conceded that Meer Alum's request to have the Governor-General's brother in command of his troops was a reason, but he had learnt this privately. In the eyes of the army and his friends at home, he had apparently been degraded. He trusted that Harris would make public why Colonel Wellesley had been appointed to a superior command.

Harris tried to smooth things over. Wellesley's appointment was political and had nothing to do with command in the field. It had been part of an agreement with the Nizam that the contingent be commanded by a colonel. He assured Baird that he would be placed in a command more suited to his rank at the first opportunity.

On this, Baird commented privately that had Wellesley been a major-general, pay and allowances would probably have been adjusted to meet that situation. But officially he let the matter rest. It was his first collision with the up-and-coming Wellesley and had it been the last would have been forgotten. But before leaving the matter it is interesting to take a closer look at the manipulative skill of Wellesley and the reactions and public statements of Harris.

A letter from Wellesley to Mornington when the Army was preparing to take the field shows that the appointment of officers to commands was not made by Harris but by a board at Madras.

"I told Clive all this," he writes, "and particularly stated to him the necessity for giving the General the credit at least for the appointments if he did not allow him to make them. It is impossible to make him too respectable or place him too high, if he is to be the head of the army in the field. This want of respectability, which is to be attributed in a large measure to the General himself, is what I am most afraid of. However, I have lectured him well on the subject, and I have publicly urged to the army (in which I flatter myself I have some influence), the necessity of supporting him whether he is right or wrong."

This gives a remarkable picture of the Commander-in-Chief of an army. He has no say in who are to have responsible posts but is allowed to pretend he has. He is not respected by the army. He even allows himself to be 'lectured' by a young colonel on how to conduct himself. It is, in short, the portrait of a 'front man' taking orders from Mornington and Clive. And as Wellesley was, by all the evidence, in control of Clive, he was able to choose for himself whatever military appointment he wanted, so long as it could be called 'political'.

The line between military and political was a fine one and without the knowledge of both, acquired in early life, Wellesley could not have risen to the heights he did. It is also important to note in the present instance that, before the army marched out of Vellore on 11th February, Mornington appointed a Committee of four colonels to advise General Harris on political matters and that one was his brother Arthur, the others being Close, Malcolm and Agnew (Harris' secretary).

Harris' orders were to march to Seringapatam and dictate terms to the enemy. If they were not accepted he was to take the place by storm. He was to try to bypass the string of hill forts captured by Cornwallis and avoid a direct clash with the enemy en route.

His two great problems were time and supplies. Victory must be achieved before the monsoons set in. If the supply system failed, the army would face starvation and defeat. Supplies depended on bullocks. The army had 96,000 while private individuals were said to have twice that number. They moved the baggage, the food, the guns, the ammunition. They carried the vast quantities of wares for sale in the travelling bazaar, equivalent in size to a large town. They provided an important part of food for the 37,000 soldiers. Their ponderous steps governed the pace of the advance. They had to be protected at all times. The caravan in motion, which included 200,000 men, women and children, covered a huge rectangle 7 miles by 3 miles. The infantry marched at the sides; at front and rear the cavalry ranged.

Of the events in the slow advance it is enough to say that after failing in an attempt to destroy a force of 6,000 men of the Bombay Army approaching from the East under General James Stuart, Tipu suffered severe casualties in an engagement with the main army at Malavelly and retired to his fortress, his mind shadowed with forebodings of impending disaster.

Harris reached his objective on 3rd April and took up a strong position to the west of Seringapatam. With high ground to his right, deep ravines to the rear and on his left the River Cauvery and an aqueduct, the only possible danger was from the woods and rocky hills to his front - and this only from snipers and rocket men. He thought he had adequate supplies of food and ammunition. His siege train had been brought up and he was at the right spot to link up with Stuart's Bombay Army.

On 4th April began the curious happenings in the Sultanpettah Tope, the woods to the right of the Army which had to be cleared of the enemy before an advance could be made to the site intended for the main assault. Baird was ordered to carry out this operation under cover of darkness with a party from his Brigade, although by a strange oversight he was not told to remain in occupation. The trees were of betel nut palm and the area crossed by irrigation ditches several feet deep, all of which had to be negotiated in darkness and in the face of possible enemy fire. Entering the woods with his party he was surprised at meeting no resistance and after combing the area, concluded the enemy had retreated and ordered a return to camp.

Next day, when the Army prepared to advance, it found the enemy had again taken up positions in the Tope. In spite of Baird's report of the difficulties encountered, Harris ordered Wellesley with the 33rd and a native infantry regiment to take and hold the Tope, again under cover of darkness, while Colonel Shawe with the 12th captured the enemy posts to the left. Having dined with Harris, Wellesley, in what appears to be a strange blunder, set off into a wall of blackness with the fires and lights of the camp lighting up his advance. He had scarcely entered the wood at the head of the light company of the 33rd, when they came under fire at once from many quarters. There was instant confusion with his men, already separated from the main body, forming into detached groups and firing on each other.

Wellesley found himself isolated with Captain McKenzie of the Madras Engineers and the two wandered aimlessly for several hours until, by good fortune, they arrived back in camp. Making his way to Headquarters in a state of great agitation, Wellesley reported to Harris who later expressed his opinion that 'it must have been particularly unpleasant for him'.

Others were less charitable. Losing contact with his men was easily explained. But returning without them and doing nothing to retrieve the situation was another matter. Had he not been the Governor General's brother, few doubted he would have had to answer to a court-martial. Among the critics was Major Shee, Wellesley's second-in-command who did not always see eye to eye with his senior. Shee managed to round up most of the 33rd and the native regiment and bring them back to camp. He was surprised to find his C.O. 'locked in the arms of Morpheus' on the table where he had dined with General Harris a few hours before.

The failure to take the Tope was a set-back to the tight schedule. Time would not allow another night attack. The obstacle had to be removed at once and, to retrieve his reputation, Wellesley was given command of the Scotch Brigade and a native battalion to carry out the operation. Colonel Shawe, who had successfully performed his mission, was sent orders to attack at the same time from the advance posts on the left.

The assault party assembled at dawn but of Wellesley there was no sign. Harris, becoming increasingly apprehensive, began to pace up and down, enquiring of his staff what could have delayed the Colonel. At last, deciding the operation must proceed, he turned to Baird and ordered him to take over command. Baird at once drew his sword and turning his horse, rode towards the waiting troops. He had only gone a few paces when Harris called him back and said. "I think, on reflection, we must wait a little longer for Colonel Wellesley."

Baird immediately said how pleased he was, adding – "it could only be painful to Colonel Wellesley if any other person was employed to complete the operation he had begun." A few minutes later Wellesley appeared and successfully led the attack.[1]

So all ended well for him. Yet a mystery still hangs over his lateness. Officially it was said that the Adjutant-General's office failed to warn him for the duty. This is strange, for the Adjutant-General was Barry Close, a personal friend of Wellesley, and according to Mornington, 'by far the ablest man in the army'.

See Appendix 1

CHAPTER 8

India. Conquest of Seringapatam.

Tipu made no attempt at compromise before the Grand Army had marched and had not replied to a letter from Mornington sent to him by Harris as he crossed the Mysore frontier. Now the Army was taking up positions for the final assault on his Capital, he broke his silence.

> "I have adhered to treaties. What is the meaning of the English armies and the occurrence of hostilities. Inform me. What need I say more?"

Harris replied by referring Tipu to Mornington's letters which, he said, explained the reasons for the British presence.

Stuart's Bombay Army arrived on the 14th. It was short of supplies, and supplies suddenly loomed as Harris' main worry. Instead of the supposed month's rations, there was found to be only enough for two weeks. Later it was said that food had been hi-jacked to be sold at inflated prices. Whatever the cause, the need to bring the campaign to a conclusion was imperative and efforts to breach the East wall of the fort went on at a frenzied pace.

On 20th, Tipu despatched his last despairing letter, requesting a conference. Harris replied with a list of conditions for peace. Four of Tipu's sons and four of his generals must be handed over as hostages, all his French advisers dismissed, half his kingdom surrendered and an enormous indemnity paid.

Tipu did not bother to reply.

On 2nd May the batteries set up a concentrated bombardment of the spot chosen for the breach in the south east corner of the ramparts. Twenty four hours later the assault was considered practicable.

Baird had volunteered to lead the storming party, an offer which Harris could hardly have refused. But he was still excluded from the councils of the Commission appointed by Mornington to advise Harris. Of the 5,000 troops detailed for the assault, three fifths were European. They were to advance in two columns, each led by a forlorn hope of a sergeant and 12 volunteers, followed by 25 men under a lieutenant. The columns were to separate at the breach, the left to advance along the ramparts under Colonel Dunlop, the right under Colonel Sherbrooke.

The assault was timed for 1 p.m., the hottest hour of the day and the one calculated as the least expected. Baird was to get his men into the trenches in small parties, a task that would keep him occupied most of the night. As the men filed past he recognised several of his old Regiment and even a few survivors from captivity. To these he spoke with particular encouragement, saying they would soon have the chance 'to pay off old scores'.

For him it was to be the day of final reckoning. He too had old scores to settle and could hardly fail to see himself in the role of Nemesis. His men would fight savagely. The hours of waiting would see to that. They would be hungry, for there was no proper arrangement to feed them in the trenches. But, like all armies of the day, they were used to fighting on empty stomachs.

Bathed in sweat, their clothes tight to their bodies, they waited as the sun beat down with increasing intensity. Their nerves frayed by the roar of the guns that pounded the breach, they cursed everything in general and swore revenge for the cruelties inflicted on their comrades in the prisons of Mysore.

But most of all their talk turned to loot, the fabulous riches that lay within the walls of the Palace.

At ten minutes past one, Baird stepped out of the front trench, his sword raised.

"Men! Are you ready?"

An answering roar.

"Then follow me, lads."

The forlorn hope raced for the breach. The men heaved themselves out of the trenches and ran in untidy columns the 1,000 yards to the river. At the 300 yards crossing that had been marked with sticks the night before, they came in full view of the defenders. Under concentrated fire from cannon, musket and rocket, the columns began to stray from the markers, moving instinctively into deeper water and the protection of the banks of an old water tank.

Seeing this, Baird, who was leading the left column, moved into the centre of the ford, making himself the focal point for his own men and the enemy alike. With shot spattering around him he walked steadily for the bank, reaching it with the head of the column and hard on the heels of the forlorn hope. The ditch, almost filled with rubble, was easily crossed in the face of heavy fire. A survivor of the forlorn hope climbed the ramparts and hoisted the flag to loud cheers, echoed by the spectators in the British camp. From trenches to ramparts had taken just six minutes.

The columns scrambled through the breach, separating to right and left, with Baird attaching himself to Sherbrooke's in its advance along the southern ramparts. Meeting little resistance and delaying only to leave detachments at each strong point, the front column arrived at the East Gate, the pre-arranged rendezvous with Dunlop's men. There Baird ordered a halt for rest and to assess the situation.

The progress of the left column had been more eventful. A party of the 12th Regiment under Captain Goodall used some scaffolding left by the defenders to cross the ditch between the outer and inner ramparts. These men then proceeded along the inner rampart and, although disobeying orders, were destined to play a vital role in the fight.

The main part of the column succeeded in taking the bastion at the north east corner but travelling 300 yards along the rampart, was brought to a halt by sustained fire from a traverse. Signs of disarray began to appear, for which there were two main reasons. Dunlop had been put out of action at the breach and several senior officers killed or wounded; and the grenadiers were unsettled from their powder being wet after straying into deep water at the crossing. Lieutenant Farquhar, the officer responsible for marking the crossing the night before, made strenuous efforts to rally the men. He was partially successful and about to lead the advance when he was shot dead. Fortunately more troops arrived and the defenders began to give way.

As the advance gained momentum, the retreat of the Mysoreans turned to panic and a headlong rush for the imagined safety of the fort. The pursuit continued up to the North Gate, where the presence of Goodall's men on the inner rampart turned the rout into a massacre, with the Mysoreans caught in a murderous fire from front and rear, the dead choking up the gateway and the living unable to move.

At the East Gate, Baird could hear the firing distinctly and when it died down, expecting to be joined by Dunlop's men, he turned his attention to securing the person of Tipu who he suspected had retired to his Palace. Believing this would be strongly defended, he told Major Allan to inform those inside that further resistance would be useless. If they surrendered unconditionally they would be given full protection; but if these terms were not accepted the Palace would be attacked and no quarter given.

No sooner had Allan gone than Baird was approached by Colonel Close with disturbing news. He had been told that all prisoners taken in the campaign had been executed on Tipu's orders - the 12 grenadiers taken in the Tope having been murdered by nails driven into their heads. Although Baird found the story hard to believe, he ordered Close to make further enquiries, commenting to Colonel Wallace of the 74th that, if it was true and Tipu taken alive, he would hand him over to the grenadiers of the 33rd to be tried for murder.

Allan had meanwhile arrived at the Palace to find Major Shee with men of the 33rd looking up at the balcony, where several of Tipu's family with officials and servants were standing in a state of fear. Fastening a white cloth on a sergeant's pike, he managed to persuade the Kellidar to allow him, with two officers, to climb the wall into the Palace. Surrounded by Palace guards, he questioned the Kellidar as to the whereabouts of his Master. That official continued to maintain that, although all the Sultan's family was in the Palace, the Sultan was not.

Allan then asked to see the princes and, when consent was reluctantly given, he entered a room to find them seated on a carpet waiting to receive him. Recognising the eldest boy, Moize U'Deen, from when he had been taken hostage by Cornwallis, and seeing how he and his brothers were trying to hide their fears, he took them by the hand and tried to reassure him that no harm would come to him. He then begged the boy to tell him where his father was hidden, as only by giving himself up could his life be saved.

Receiving repeated denials, Allan asked for the gates to be opened. At this there was great consternation. He was told such a step could only be taken by the Sultan himself. Only after repeated assurance that he would remain with them and that no one would enter without his orders, was consent given.

The gates were opened to reveal the tall figure of Baird in front of a large body of troops. He ordered Close and Allan to bring the princes out to him. At this the boys displayed great fear, not only at leaving the safety of the Palace but from realising the identity of the towering figure that had now assumed control.

The events that followed had a dramatic quality which captured public imagination at the time and continued to do so throughout the Victorian era. In Allan's words, Baird was 'justly excited' by the report he had received of the murders of the prisoners and this was probably heightened by 'a momentary recollection of his own sufferings in that place.' The princes, small, with the delicate beauty often seen in the Indian boy, were depicted as innocent victims on the altar of their father's iniquities.

The reality was different. Baird hesitated before reassuring the boys. But as he explained in his report, this was only to see if their fears would persuade them to tell him where their father was. After a few minutes 'he was sensibly affected at the sight of the princes and repeatedly assured them that no violence would be offered to them'. He waited until they were more composed before handing them over to Colonel Agnew, to be escorted to General Harris in the British

Camp.

He then entered the Palace and, after ordering the guards to be disarmed, had the place thoroughly searched for the Sultan. The questioning of officials continued until at last the Kellidar began to show signs of agitation and blurted out that he had heard the Sultan was lying severely wounded in the gateway of the fort. Baird at once set off with a search party for the Northern Gate, into which the panic-stricken Mysoreans had been funnelled by Dunlop's column and was still piled high with the bodies of the dead and dying.

Body after body was dragged from the pile, to be identified by the Kellidar. As darkness fell, Baird ordered flares to be brought and the gruesome search went on. At last a wounded man identified himself as one of Tipu's servants and pointed to the spot where his master lay. By the flickering light of the flares a body was extracted from the heap and carried to the Kellidar. By the short, stout frame, the high shoulders, the small hands and feet and, even in death, the expression 'of stern composure, distinguishing him above the common order of people' - there could be no doubt it was the Sultan.

The story of his death was pieced together and it became clear he had died the death of a soldier. As soon as the assault began, probably in despair, he had abandoned his role of general and taken command of the traverse at which the left column had met much stiff resistance. His guns silenced, he had mounted his horse and made for the Northern Gate where he arrived already wounded and so hemmed in by his followers that escape was impossible. Wounded in his chest and his horse shot under him, he fell unnoticed by all but his attendants, who tried in vain to drag him to safety.

Minutes later, an unknown soldier, attracted by the glint of his richly ornamented belt, snatched at the buckle. Summoning up his last strength, Tipu dealt the man a slash with his sword across the knee. The soldier shot him through the head and passed on, oblivious of his victim's identity.[2]

Baird ordered the Sultan's body to be placed on a palanquin and taken into the Palace to lie in state. Before it went, he bent down and cut off a small pouch of velvet, saying: "I never plunder, but I will keep this as a memorial of him". He then returned to the Palace with the 33rd and 74th Regiments.

He applied to Harris for all the assault force to be withdrawn and replaced by fresh troops, better able to patrol the streets. This had not been complied with and, as night had fallen, little could be done to stop the plunder. Fatigued with his exertions of the last twenty four

See Appendix 2

hours, he placed a carpet on the verandah at the main entrance and lay there to ensure the safety of those inside the Palace. His thoughts are not hard to imagine, for history affords few examples of so extraordinary a reversal of fortune as his: after a lapse of fifteen years, a prisoner guarding the body of his one time gaoler.

He had just settled down when a messenger came in haste to tell him that the Treasury had been broken into and troops were looting the money and jewels. As a strong guard had been posted on the building, Baird sent Colonel Wallace with an escort to investigate. Wallace, finding that a door inside the Palace had been forced open into the Treasury, entered upon an amazing sight. Men were loading themselves with gold and precious ornaments, unconscious of their true value, which, if properly disposed of, would have kept them in luxury for life. Not only the men; several officers were busily involved in the plunder. One of these gentlemen, catching sight of Wallace, quickly put on a pretence of indignation and made a show of trying to stop the activity around him. With great difficulty the Treasury was cleared, though the value of the loot taken was never established.

Baird was given the names of the officers seen by Wallace and dealt with them severely. But, with the delicacy that became linked with his name, did not reveal their identities to avoid causing grief to their families.

CHAPTER 9

India. Superseded by Colonel Wellesley. 1799.

With daylight, it became possible to assess the pillage and take measures to end it. As a start, Baird ordered the Provost Marshal to proclaim publicly in all parts of the town that anyone caught looting would be hanged without trial. He then sat down with his staff to discuss further procedures for bringing life back to normal.

They had hardly begun when there was a bustle outside and Arthur Wellesley walked in. Marching up to Baird he presented him with a paper and said briskly:

"General Baird, I am appointed to the command of Seringapatam and here is the order of General Harris."

There was a moment of incredulous silence. Then Baird stood up and turning to his staff, said:

"Come gentlemen, we no longer have any business here."

As the party rose from the table, Wellesley interjected:

"Oh, pray finish your breakfast."

Disdaining to reply, Baird strode out of the room followed by his staff.

It would require a minute search of the annals of warfare to find so callous a removal of a general from his command in his hour of victory. Did Wellesley have no qualms? Apparently not. He seems to have taken pride in the way he gave Baird his marching orders, for the above account is based on the one he gave George Elers, who happened to be a friend of Baird's.[3]

Lord Roberts (Bobs) in his book, *Rise of Wellington*, more than a century later, expresses the feelings of all career soldiers when he stresses Wellesley's lack of sensitivity and points out that 'he does not seem to have realised that Baird had been treated badly, or that he himself owed his exceptional advancement to his relationship with the Governor-General'.

Baird's bitter disappointment is summed up in a letter to a friend:

"Before the sweat was dry on my brow, I was superseded by an inferior officer."

That it should be an 'inferior', that is junior officer, was the crux of the matter. Had he been replaced by one of his two seniors in the army, assuming either had been willing, he would have had little cause for complaint. But no major-general would have been content

See Appendix 3

to have a lieutenant-colonel 'put over his head'.

Baird believed that, in ordinary justice, he should have been allowed to restore order in the place he had taken. That he would have carried it out as efficiently as Wellesley is demonstrated beyond doubt by his subsequent achievements, but that was what the Commission, through Harris, wanted to avoid. He also thought that he should have had the honour of handing over the town to Harris.

Which raises the question of where was Harris?

He was not in the town the day it was captured and, in the following days, seems to have taken little interest in what was going on there. His explanation of how he came to replace Baird is ironical, when it is known that all such decisions were made by the Commission. He said he received a request from Baird to be relieved and asked his Deputy Adjutant-General to name the next officer for duty.

"Colonel Roberts," he was told.

"Then put him in orders to go," said Harris.

Soon after, the D A-G, "looking more attentively at the order," said,

"No, Sir, I have made a mistake; Colonel Wellesley is the next for duty, not Colonel Roberts."

"Then let Colonel Wellesley be put in orders for the relief," said Harris.

If this is to be believed, Harris had not yet decided on a permanent commander and Wellesley took over from Baird expecting to be relieved himself in due course. He said his mind was made up by a letter from Wellesley on 6th May, which began:

"Plunder is stopped — the fires are out and the inhabitants are returning to their houses fast."

The letter also stressed the need to appoint a permanent garrison and commanding officer. That Wellesley knew the appointment would be his is shown in his concluding paragraph:

"In hopes you will attend to my recommendations to send a garrison tomorrow. I'll look out a place to accommodate one or two battalions of Europeans and three or four sepoys."

Harris carried out his instructions and appointed Wellesley permanently to the command.

The day after the assault, without consulting Baird, Harris rushed out a General Order congratulating the Army on its great victory. He referred in some detail to the operation and thanked Baird 'in the warmest terms ..... for the decided and able manner in which he conducted the assault and the humane measures which he had subsequently adopted for preserving order.'

He praised several officers, including Colonel Dunlop, but did not mention Sherbrooke. This showed he had received no precise information on the operations, as Dunlop had been put out of action at the breach while Sherbrooke had been with his column throughout. Baird, who had no time to make out his official report whilst in command, rectified Harris' misinformation on the day after he was superseded.

> "I perceive in the General Order of yesterday that no mention is made of Colonel Sherbrooke. This, I presume, is owing to the order being published before I had time to make a report to you on the conduct of the troops under my command in the assault ..... and if, where all behaved nobly, it is proper to mention individual merit, I know no man so justly entitled to praise as Colonel Sherbrooke, to whose exertions I feel indebted for the success of the attack."

Two days later Harris published an awkward amendment to his Order in which he quoted the last, though not of course the first part, of the above extract.

By this time he had also received a letter from Baird protesting at his supersession.

Having carried out the assault to General Harris' satisfaction, he had naturally concluded that he would be allowed to retain the command of Seringapatam, or at least would not have been superseded by a junior officer. He had been reinforced in this belief by Harris' repeated assurances that he would be placed in a situation more suited to his rank at the first opportunity. But after this second supersession he felt that His Majesty and the Commander-in-Chief in England would be led to believe he was not fit for any command of importance.

He had not, as was rumoured, asked to be relieved of the command, and this Harris well knew. He had only asked to be relieved for a short time, to have the honour of reporting the particulars of the assault to Harris in person. But, as this had not been found convenient, he had sent an officer at dawn the following day to say that he wished to remain to examine the effects of the assault. The officer had returned and reported that Harris had received his message long before Colonel Wellesley arrived at the Palace.

In conclusion, he requested that copies of his letter be forwarded to the Duke of York for the information of His Majesty and 'that at the same time he is informed of my having been twice superseded by Colonel Wellesley, he may be in possession of such reasons as you may think proper to give for it, that he may be satisfied the measure was dictated by necessity and not from any want of capacity on my part to fill the situation'.

Two days later Baird received a reply from Colonel Agnew, Harris's secretary, which suggests that the General was too unsure of himself to deal with the issue in a straightforward manner and was leaving it to the Commission, of which Agnew was a member, to sort out.

The General considered Baird's letter to be 'very improper and that no officer who thought himself authorised to remonstrate with his superior could be usefully employed in the army he commanded'. Baird 'had his permission to proceed by the first conveyance to Fort St. George'. The General would certainly forward his letter to the Duke of York together with his reply.

Baird received Agnew's letter 'with the greatest astonishment'. He had given 'the most respectful statement of facts about his supersession as would any military man in a similar situation'. He had read his letter over and over again but had found no paragraph, or even a word 'which could be misconstrued into the smallest disrespect'. However, as one who abhorred the crime of insubordination, he trusted General Harris would give him the chance to clear himself before a court-martial.

As to leaving the army, he was only too anxious to do so as soon as there was no chance it would be actively employed. But if General Harris persisted in ordering him from the army, he regretted the necessity of making it, and the circumstances that accompanied it, equally public.

This second letter naturally produced no change in Harris' position.

'It was', wrote Agnew, 'not the words but the tone of the letter that invoked the General's comments. General Harris hoped that this reply would conclude a correspondence which Baird was at liberty to make as public as he thought proper.'

The ball was now back in Baird's court, and he was evidently at a loss how to return it. Resentment at his supersession, as Harris's advisers had shrewdly guessed, was being replaced by the spectre of insubordination.

At such times he was not one to mull over his grievances to the exclusion of all else. He never lost sleep in times of stress, having the ability (also attributed to Wellington) of being able to drop off at will. Nor was he one to take it out of those under him.

He had on his staff a cornet named Kippen, an inquisitive young man who happened to be in Baird's tent when he was answering some letters from home. Becoming aware that the cornet was peeping over his shoulder, Baird picked up some unread letters and holding them out, said: "Here, Mr. Kippen, are some of a more recent date."

Kippen retired red faced, while Baird watched him go with amusement.*

Meanwhile, other events had begun to impinge on the supersession issue. All fourteen field officers who had taken part in the assault decided to show their regard for Baird by ordering a dress sword from England (value 200 guineas) bearing the following inscription:

"SERINGAPATAM, taken by storm on 4th May 1799.

Presented by the Field Officers who personally served under Major-General Baird on that occasion."†

In a letter on their behalf, Colonel Sherbrooke asked Baird to do them the honour of accepting it 'as a mark of their esteem and of their admiration of his personal exertions on that day'.

Next, Wellesley stepped in by sending Tipu's sword to Baird with a note asking him, as the one with the best title, to accept it. But now the general resentment over the supersession surfaced to frustrate this attempt at reconciliation. General Floyd, President of the Prize Committee, sent a letter to Harris requesting that the sword be returned to them as it was not Colonel Wellesley's to dispose of. The Committee intended to have the sword presented to General Baird on behalf of the whole army by the Commander-in-Chief in person.

Harris, aware of the comments circulating about his role in the supersession, must have received this letter with mixed feelings. On 8th June he directed all his officers to assemble and, in the words of his diary, 'addressed them as nearly as follows'.

"Gentlemen, I have assembled this very respectable meeting on an occasion which, I have no doubt, will give equal pleasure to all ...... Taking the sword from Scot (my A-D-C) I said, Major-General Baird, I have the pleasure to present you with the sword you have so honourably obtained, and most sincerely wish you long to wear it."

While this little speech gives an indication of Harris' command of the language, Baird's reaction is even more revealing. In Harris's own words, "General Baird was too much agitated to make any connected reply."

*George Elers repeats the story told by Kippen.

†The sword is now in the Scottish United Services Museum with other relics of Baird and Tipu Sultan.

The same evening he wrote to Harris:

"From the state of my feelings this morning I really was incapable of making any reply to the distinguished honour which the army had been pleased to present me ....." He concluded with his "warmest thanks for the very handsome manner" in which Harris had made the presentation.

His inability to speak coherently hints at pent-up emotions over recent events and memories of his long imprisonment which he affected to make light of. There is, too, the paradox of one who could face suffering and death without flinching, yet be 'too agitated to make any reply' when an honour was conferred on him.

The presentation marked the end of his official protest at the supersession. Harris destroyed the letters, doubtless with relief, but copies were found amongst Baird's papers after his death. His relations with Harris from then on were always friendly. Never one to harbour grudges, his resentment, for a time at least, appears to have been expunged by the presentation of the sword.

Yet for the army the affair was not over. Apart from the question of seniority that affected every serving officer, it was going to take a long time to forgive Wellesley for taking command of Seringapatam 'without sharing the dangers of the assault'. The army also reserved for Baird another honour. As the anniversary came round, the toast included neither Harris nor Wellesley. It went:

'BAIRD AND THE HEROES OF SERINGAPATAM.'

That Harris was disturbed by the resentment caused by his decision to remove Baird is shown in a letter to Mornington on 28th June. Protesting that he had 'acted from the heart' he said that if it was worthwhile to defend his Lordship's brother's appointment against the nonsense talked by ill-intentioned people, he could do so 'on principles most militarily correct'.

Mornington hastened to assure him he had made the right decision. As Harris well knew, he never recommended his brother to him or suggested how, or where, he should be employed. But because of his brother's 'discretion, judgement, temper and integrity', if Harris had not placed him in Seringapatam, he would have done so himself.

With the true relationship of the characters involved in mind, the irony in this word play is obvious.

Harris did not have to bear the strain of office much longer. The same year he returned to England with his share of the prize money, a large sum of £142,000. There was much comment at his insistence on receiving the last penny, and comparison was made with Cornwallis and Medows in the 1792 Campaign. Of those who risked their lives in the assault, Baird received the most - £1,200.

Two years later, when attending one of the Duke of York's levees at the Horse Guards, Harris was asked without warning by the Duke:

"Pray, General Harris, what reason had you for superseding General Baird in the command of Seringapatam and giving it to a junior officer?"

Harris stammered and was at a loss for an answer so the Duke turned his back on him and began a conversation with some other officers.*

Perhaps, after all, it was as well for Harris that Baird did not press for their correspondence to be forwarded to the Duke.

*George Elers.

CHAPTER 10

India. Supersedes Colonel Wellesley. 1801.

On Wellesley's own admission, Seringapatam was the base on which his reputation was founded. By the same token, the opportunity was denied to Baird. Whether he would have been a failure, as Wellesley's admirers have asserted, is impossible to say.

What is not in doubt is that he would not have enjoyed Wellesley's enormous advantage through his relationship with the Governor-General, which gave him a freedom of action beyond any that Baird could have hoped for.

He strongly objected to Mornington's avowed intention of coming to Seringapatam to 'settle things'. His brother could make the decisions at Madras, leaving those on the spot to carry out his orders. He wanted to get rid of Harris and his army, which was a 'menace to good order'. Plundering was still going on, creating terror amongst the inhabitants. (A surprising admission this, since only two days before he had assured Harris that plunder had stopped and everything was returning to normal).

He refused to share responsibility with any civil servant and threatened that, if any were appointed not directly under his orders, he would ask to be withdrawn with the army. By the end of August his fears were allayed. The main army had gone and so had the generals. Most intended to sail for home, though Baird decided to stay. It was not a wise decision. He had lost out to the Wellesleys and the factors which persuaded him to stay, his knowledge of South India and his reputation in the army, were just the ones that would tell against him. As Wellesley's senior he remained a threat, and could expect no favours from the Governor-General.

Yet, still judging others by his own standards, he returned to Madras and called at Government House unsuspecting of what lay in store. As he entered Mornington appeared on the stairway. The little man hesitated a moment, then, his face lighting up, he ran down to embrace the large frame of the somewhat embarrassed soldier.

This preliminary over, they sat down while Mornington enthused over Baird's achievement. All Madras was singing the praises of the gallant victor of Seringapatam. Soon the whole British nation would be joining in. He would personally recommend that Baird receive a financial reward commensurate with the great service he had rendered the nation. He would put forward his name for the K.B.

But that lay in the future. There was now the question of how he should be employed. Did he have anything in mind? Baird suggested that as his friend, General Floyd, was leaving for England, he would like nothing better than to take over the command of the Southern Division.

Ah, yes. That vacancy would soon arise. But, and here Mornington's tone was one of regret, "the appointment of Floyd's successor was in the giving of Lord Clive and, as General Baird probably knew, he never interfered in his Lordship's affairs. However, if Baird applied to Lord Clive, he would certainly support his application. Alternatively, if Baird would come to Calcutta, he could choose any command he liked in the Bengal Presidency.

For Baird the choice was easy. All his service had been in the South where he was well known. He said he would apply for Floyd's command.

Now the truth of the situation emerged. Clive, with none of Mornington's skill at dissembling, failed to disguise the fact that far from supporting the application, the Governor-General wanted Baird removed from the Presidency.

Left with no alternative, Baird sailed for Calcutta where Mornington had just preceded him. He was received with the same effusive concern for his well being. But when he reminded Mornington of his promise of a choice of commands, the response was again one of regret. There was at the moment only one vacancy, and that of no great importance, at Dinapore. Baird was forced to accept and left with Mornington's continued protestations of concern for his welfare.

He had been at Dinapore about a year when rumours of preparations for a military expedition against either Batavia or Mauritius began to circulate. He wrote at once to Sir Alured Clarke, C-in-C at Calcutta, for confirmation and, should the rumours be correct, asking for the command of the force taking part. Clarke replied that an expedition was indeed planned and added that he had recommended Baird for the command but had been over-ruled by the Governor-General, who reserved the right to appoint the officers taking part.

Baird asked for leave to make a personal application to Mornington. Clarke, who was Deputy Governor-General as well as C-in-C, and had often chafed at the way his recommendations in military matters had been overridden, not only acceded, but told Baird he could quote him as his source of information.

In his previous brushes with authority Baird had used letters. He had argued his case well but the trump cards had always been with his superiors. Now he was to try the personal approach, one for which he was eminently qualified.* He was received cordially as ever, but Mornington, aware of the subject Baird wanted to raise, kept up a barrage of small talk and as Baird, after taking his leave remarked, "every subject under the sun seemed to have been touched on but one — the expeditionary force assembling in South India."

He returned to his quarters where he was given a piece of news that made his hackles rise. The commander of the force *had* been appointed and was none other than Colonel Wellesley. Determined to have the matter out once and for all, he demanded and obtained another interview with Mornington.

He began by asking bluntly if it was true that Colonel Wellesley had been given the command. If that was so, he was again to be superseded by the same junior officer. He had been promoted major-general and ordered to India from the Cape by the Horse Guards and must have been considered fit to perform the duties of an officer of that rank. Yet since his arrival he had been systematically denied commands that were available, some of which had been given to a regimental officer.

Mornington angrily replied that he had no intention of answering questions about the proposed expedition. It was his responsibility and his alone.

Baird, equally incensed, retorted that as Mornington well knew he was not concerned with the details of the expedition. He wanted, and had a right to know who was to command it. He had not come to ask favours. He was pressing his claims as a major-general on the staff against those of an inferior officer.

The argument continued and even as tempers cooled, agreement seemed as far away as ever. At last, Baird, feeling that further protest was useless, was about to leave with the parting shot — "Am I to take it then My Lord, that I am not to command or be employed on this expedition?"

To his surprise, Mornington hesitated. Then, suddenly reverting to his usual conciliatory tones, asked Baird to remain in Calcutta until he had heard from him.

Next day, on instructions from Clarke, Baird called again on the Governor-General and was told he was to command the expedition. What, then, had caused Mornington to change his mind? Admittedly, Baird in determined mood was not an easy man to brush aside. But added to this was the weight of army opinion. Exactly how this was applied is not certain. Clarke as C-in-C harboured a personal

*This is Colonel Thornton's opinion in *Light and Shade in Bygone India*.

grievance and Sir James Craig, Commander of the Upper Provinces, was believed to have written a letter to be forwarded to the Duke of York, protesting at Mornington's continued appointing of his brother to posts he was not entitled to by his rank. But resentment at Mornington's nepotism extended beyond the generals. Every officer outside the Wellesley circle felt the threat to his prospects of advancement.

It is remarkable how supersession was to link and scar the lives of Baird and Wellesley. Baird had already suffered. Now it was Wellesley's turn, a fact of which Mornington was well aware. Before Baird left Calcutta he received a confidential letter which, after the usual buttering up, went:

> "I have chosen my brother to second you in this glorious enterprise; and rely on your giving the public the full benefits of his talents by admitting him to your cordial confidence, and by uniting most harmoniously and zealously with him in the prosecution of my wishes ..... ."

Baird replied:

> "Your Lordship may rest assured that everything in my power shall be done to promote and maintain harmony in the army of which you have honoured me with the command; and particularly with your brother for whom I entertain the most sincere regard."
>
> " ..... Equally unnecessary is it for me to reassure your Lordship that the talents of your brother, as well of every officer in the army shall have full scope. Trust me, My Lord, I harbour no little jealousy."

On 5th February 1801, he embarked on the *Phoenix* and waited in Saugar Roads for his final orders. Mornington's scheme included the capture of Batavia from the Dutch and Mauritius from the French. When Batavia was taken, Baird was to remain as Lieutenant-Governor with part of the expeditionary force. Wellesley would then sail for Mauritius and, when that was captured, take up a similar appointment.

Had these schemes materialised, the careers of the two leaders would have been completely changed. But the enormous time-lag in communications between England and India was to make a mockery of the carefully laid plans. Many months before the events just narrated, a decision had been made in London by Henry Dundas, the Minister for War, news of which reached Calcutta on 6th February and was conveyed to Baird in an urgent message telling him to delay sailing and expect 'some essential variations in the objectives of the expedition'.

After waiting four days he was told that the original plan was shelved. He was to assist Sir Ralph Abercrombie in driving the French out of Egypt.*

His first objective, however, would be to catch up with the army Wellesley was mobilising in Southern India. Arrived at Trincomallee on 23rd February, he found that Wellesley had read the orders from London and, acting on his own initiative, had sailed nine days before to Bombay with the transports. At Point de Galle, having missed his man by a day, he was about to resume the chase when a letter from Wellesley arrived. Explaining that he had left Trincomallee to expedite the transports, he wrote that he had only just heard of the change in command.

Baird's reply could have done nothing to soothe his old rival.

> "It is much to be regretted that you had not remained at Trincomallee until my arrival, or until you had received some of your brother's letters after my appointment to the command ....."

Urging Wellesley to embark as many troops as possible before the season of prevailing winds made it impossible to reach Suez, he concluded: " I have the pleasure to inform you that you are appointed second-in-command."

He reached Bombay on 30th March to find Wellesley had gone down with a fever. To the patient's surprise Baird went at once to visit him, showed concern at his condition and for the next few days paid him regular visits. Wellesley had awaited his arrival with some trepidation and was at once grateful and confused. His illness has since been diagnosed as psychosomatic, a reaction to supersession. Yet, on the evidence, it seems likely that he was just taken ill and became depressed by the news, particularly as he would have to serve under Baird.

This is supported by a letter he wrote to his friend Close the day he left Trincomallee, before he heard of his supersession. He said that he was hoping to return to Mysore and would receive his successor 'with great satisfaction'. Yet when the news broke, he found it impossible to be objective and, far from receiving his successor 'with satisfaction', was uncertain what action to take, concerned about what

*Napoleon had taken an army to Egypt in 1798. In August his fleet was destroyed by Nelson at the Battle of the Nile. After an abortive attack on Acre he had sailed for France, leaving his army in a state of disillusionment.

others would think and full of self-pity.

To his brother Henry in Calcutta, he wrote:

> "I was at the top of the tree in this country. But this supersession has ruined all my prospects founded upon any service I may have rendered."

Baird's stay at Bombay was short. He was anxious to leave for Mocha at the entrance to the Red Sea, where he hoped to catch up with the transports that had already sailed and take personal charge of events. Wellesley was showing signs of improvement and expected to sail with him. But on 3rd, he began to suffer from a painful condition known as Malabar Itch. Baird sailed on 6th expecting him to follow in a few days. By the 8th Wellesley decided this was out of the question and wrote a long letter giving the reasons for his decision.* Baird did not receive it for seven weeks, but, as it almost concludes the supersession saga, its gist may conveniently be inserted here.

After explaining that the state of his health made it impossible for him to join the expedition, he wrote:

> "I do this, I assure you, notwithstanding that I think it very probable that I shall soon hear of your being recalled ..... As I am writing on this subject, I will freely acknowledge that my regret at my being prevented from accompanying you has been greatly increased by the kind, candid and handsome manner in which you have behaved towards me; and I will confess as freely, not only that I did not expect such treatment, but that my wishes before you arrived regarding going on the expedition were directly the reverse of what they are at this moment.
>
> "I need not enter further into the subject than to entreat you will not attribute my stay to any other motive than that to which I have assigned it; and to inform you, that as I know what has been said and expected by the world in general, I propose, as well for my credit as for yours, to make it known to my friends and yours, not only the distinguished manner in which you have behaved towards me but the causes that have prevented my demonstrating my gratitude by giving you every assistance in the arduous service which you have to conduct."

These generous sentiments are obviously sincere and somewhat out of character for 'The Iron Duke'. But it was a passing phase. He did try to fulfil his promise, though in his letters, he never quite managed to swallow his pride. To his brother Henry, it was his 'disorder' together with the despatches from Europe that decided him not to go,

The *Susannah* in which Wellesley intended to sail was lost at sea with all hands.

though he added it was 'but justice to General Baird to say that his conduct towards me had by no means occasioned this determination; but that it was perfectly satisfactory'.

To Close, only two days after he had penned his letter to Baird, he wrote that the reason he intended to go was 'in deference to the Governor-General's wishes. But when 'upon the point of carrying into execution this laudable but highly disagreeable intention, I was seized by a fever, which kept me in bed for some days .....'.

Three months later he gave a less humiliating reason than gratitude to his old rival in a letter to Colonel Robertson:

> "I saw your friend General Baird at Bombay. When he was appointed to the command, I determined that nothing would induce me to go, for reasons which must be perfectly well known. But when the General came, he was so desirous I should accompany him, and I saw so plainly that he would be in some degree embarrassed if I did not go, that I altered my original determination. However, sickness stopped me at last."

Reading these letters one cannot fail to be impressed by the equivocation and pettiness they reveal. Perhaps such egotism is essential for a man to achieve supreme greatness: perhaps the magnanimity that was so much a part of Baird is an impediment to greatness as the world knows it.

Having gained the command, all Baird's resentment over past injustices was erased. Mornington had asked him to confirm the officers on Wellesley's staff 'in active and honourable stations'. He promised to do all he could, but hoped Mornington would understand that he must have some of his own confidential staff about him. The problem seems to have resolved itself. According to Wellesley, all his staff disliked Baird. At all events they turned down his offers — which was just as well. In the months ahead there would be no room for friction in the army.

Two of Baird's staff are of interest because of the turn of events that would bring them on a collision course many years later: his military secretary, Captain George Molle of the Scotch Brigade and his Deputy Adjutant-General and head of staff, Major Lachlan Macquarie of the 77th. Macquarie had not known Baird personally, but had been with the Bombay army at Seringapatam and watched as he led the assault. He was surprised and delighted to have been chosen.

Wellesley expressed his belief, privately, that Macquarie lacked decisiveness. But Baird, who picked him 'as a good man of business', was proved right.

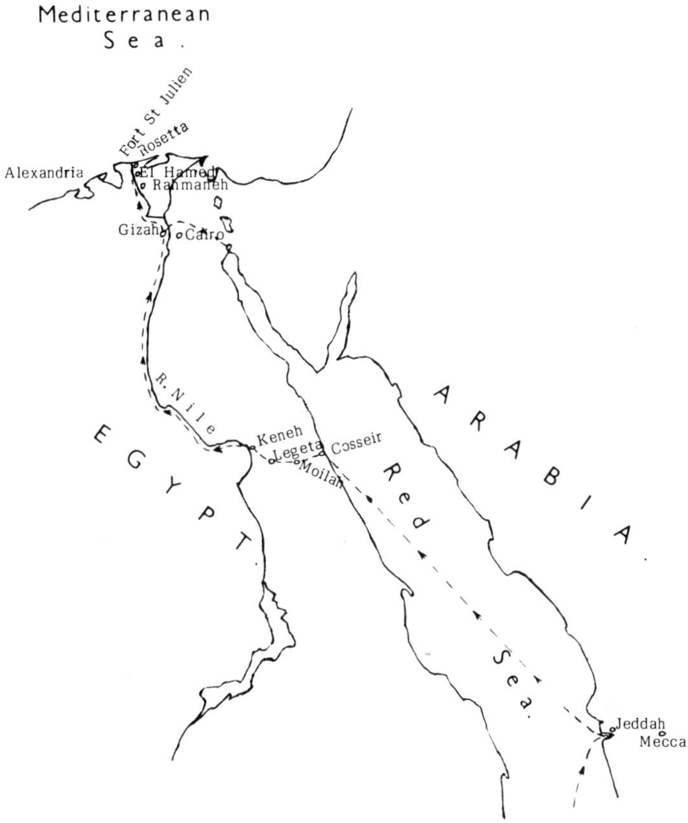

BAIRD'S ADVANCE INTO EGYPT

CHAPTER 11

Egypt. The desert crossing. 1801.

The expedition on which Baird now embarked has been branded by military historians as one of the most hare-brained ever conceived. Planned by Henry Dundas, the War Minister, its aim was to link up with another army sent to invade Egypt from the Mediterranean. How the junction of the two armies was to be effected was left entirely to the military commanders.

For Baird, the prospect was particularly daunting. He had taken over an organisation intended for a different objective, had no idea whether the army in the Mediterranean, commanded by Sir Ralph Abercromby, could land in Egypt and, if so, whether it would succeed without him or be defeated before he arrived.

Of the 6,000 men detailed for the expedition, not a single unit was yet under his control. The Bombay army and another under Colonel Beresford had already sailed. A force from the Cape was said to be coming with a naval escort commanded by Sir Home Popham. A large part of the army would be sepoys whose religion forbade their serving outside their own Country. Their conduct was therefore unpredictable. For information on his route and news of the Mediterranean army, Baird had to rely on Admiral Blankett who was *somewhere* in the 600 mile reaches of the Red Sea, taking soundings in waters unknown to Europeans, as, until recently, that part of the world had been closed to them by the Arabs.

Time was of the essence. If the forces could be assembled before the seasonal northerlies set in, they could sail to Suez and march the 70 miles desert crossing to join Abercromby. If not, the staging point would have to be Cosseir. That would entail a march, vaguely estimated as 100 miles, to the Nile across one of the most arid deserts in the world, followed by a 300 mile journey down the River to Lower Egypt, a venture unprecedented in British military history.

At Mocha, where he arrived on 25th April, Baird found that Colonel Murray, the Commissioner for the Area, had sent on the Bombay contingent and sailed himself, leaving a civilian in charge. Beresford had also sailed on. Both Murray and Beresford were known as men of initiative and Baird could only hope they would refrain from a foolhardy attack on Cosseir, which was thought to be still in French hands.

Though anxious to follow, he had first to negotiate with native rulers and officials who were, not without reason, suspicious of all Euro-

SIR HOME RIGGS POPHAM

peans' intentions. 'Proud, haughty and disdainful of foreigners', was how the Count de Noe, a French officer serving with the 10th Regiment, saw them.*

Fortunately, Baird's manly appearance and self assurance created the right impression in their male dominated society. On the advice of the native Commissioner, he dispensed bribes in the right quarters including 300 Rupees to the harbour master, who allowed Montresor's transports to be watered in spite of rough seas.

At the next stop, Jeddah, the Sheriff of Mecca, the most powerful man in the Red Sea area, was said to have had a disagreement with Admiral Blankett and forbidden the local pilots to take British ships into the port. Though unfounded, the rumour illustrates the knife-edge uncertainty of the advance. For, without water at each port of call, the fleet would have been in dire straits.

Relieved at his welcome, Baird found two disconcerting pieces of information. Murray, from whom he was hoping to gain valuable information, had sailed on with the advance divisions and there was a letter from Admiral Blankett informing him that Abercromby had landed at Aboukir and had died in the hour of victory over a French force on 21st March.

After a friendly meeting with the Sheriff of Mecca, Baird was about to leave when the naval squadron from the Cape under Sir Home Popham sailed in with the 61st troops of the 8th Dragoons and a detachment of artillery. For Baird and Popham it was the start of an eventful partnership. That they should strike up an instant friendship appears surprising for, while Baird has been regarded as a conventional soldier, Popham was, to say the least, an unconventional naval officer.

Entering the Navy in 1778, he had engaged in mercenary enterprises outside the Service that had greatly increased his private fortune and roused the intense dislike of his superiors at the Admiralty. But he had the rare distinction of having worked amicably with the Army, notably as officer in charge of waterways in the disastrous 1794 Campaign in the Netherlands, for which he had been promoted post-captain on the recommendation of the Duke of York. A man of immense energy and resource, with a forceful and persuasive manner, he evidently found Baird a kindred spirit: a tireless worker, resourceful in an emergency and able to turn on the charm.

Like Baird he saw to the welfare of his men and, incidentally, under his leadership they knew they were in line for any prize money that was going. But his achievements as a naval officer were solid enough.

*Mémoires relatifes à l'Expédition Anglaise de l'Inde en Egypte.

He carried out valuable surveys in the Indian Ocean and invented a code of signals that remained in use in the Navy for many years.

At his request, Baird embarked on *HMS Romney* to arrive at Cosseir on June 8th. There he was relieved to find the French had evacuated the fort and his advance divisions already encamped in tents one and half miles outside the town, which according to de Noe was 'a miserable cluster of wretched hovels built with shells and mud'.

With no further news from Blankett, the lateness of the season now made sailing to Suez out of the question. An attempt would have to be made at crossing from Cosseir to Keneh on the Nile.

The difficulties to be overcome would be enormous. Supply lines stretched back across 1,000 miles of treacherous and uncharted seas. Many ships were overdue, some were known to have foundered and there had been no news of Wellesley or of the transports that were to accompany him.

The terrain could not have been more dispiriting.

"I shall never forget the deep impression of melancholy made upon my mind by the sight of this desolate coast," wrote de Noe. "The heart shuddered at the idea of even a temporary residence on its arid shores."

The rock-bound anchorage at Cosseir could take no more than five ships at a time and, at the onset of easterly winds, they had to put out to sea. In the weeks to come, it would have to cope with more than a hundred transports with troops, camp-followers, animals, guns and all the provisions of an army on the move.

Apart from all this, Baird was faced with two basic problems. After their long and enervating voyage the men had to be prepared physically and mentally to meet the challenge of the desert; and he had to ensure a constant supply of water on the march.

The Europeans were in surprisingly good condition, for which James McGrigor, the Chief Medical Officer, later paid tribute to Mornington's foresight and Baird's unceasing efforts in fitting out the ships for the voyage. The sepoys had suffered more from the unfamiliar confinement but soon recovered on the diet that was naturally more to their liking than it was to the Europeans.

Long experience and training had taught Baird the absolute necessity of keeping the men occupied to maintain discipline. He ordered regular parades and drill in spite of the heat and encouraged any other activities that could be thought up. He moved constantly among the men to keep up morale. On this de Noe says:

> "The manly figure and martial air of the General at once gained him

> the respect of the troops; and when his whole character became known to them, never did commander more completely gain the enthusiastic attachment of his men than he did."

He had the support of several talented officers though some were inclined to being temperamental. This surfaced on the arrival of the Cape contingent. With it came Colonel Samuel Auchmuty, appointed by the Horse Guards as Adjutant-General. A third generation American, he had fought on the British side in the War of Independence and, after arriving in England penniless, had risen from lieutenant entirely on merit. Baird had had him in his division at Seringapatam in 1792 and was delighted to see him. But Macquarie, who felt he was being down-graded, admitted later that, had Baird not cajoled him into staying, he would have pulled out.

Another arrival was a Dr Shapter who displaced McGrigor as head of the Medical Service. Many years later, McGrigor recalled how put out he felt and how Baird talked him over by making him personally responsible for the desert crossing. Both Macquarie and McGrigor were destined for greater things but remained close friends of Baird for the rest of their lives.

Though of vital importance for the caravans trading between Arabia and Egypt, the route from the Red Sea across the desert to the Upper Nile was unknown to the British. The march would have to be planned on information gathered locally and this, as was soon discovered, had to be treated with scepticism, not because of deception by the Arabs, but because they could not give the distances in British standards of measurement.

Only two stopping places were known to exist on the route: Moilah, estimated at 40 miles from Cosseir, Legeta another 30 miles on, with a further 30 to the Nile. While adequate for traders with their camels, it would be impossible for an army to march such distances.

Baird's first move was to send Murray with some of the Bombay contingent, including sepoys, to reconnoitre the route and establish extra stopping places for stores of army rations that would be supplemented with food bought from the natives en route. The latter was essential and it is curious to note that Baird departed from the usual custom of dealing with the Arabs, by giving strict orders that everything bought locally must be paid for on the spot. The vendors were so surprised, says de Noe, that 'they furnished when required by the Catchief or Arab officer, the different supplies very readily'.

All possible ways of carrying the water on the march were considered and finally reduced to either casks or skin bags (puckallies or musacks) slung over the backs of camels. Casks were eliminated when found to warp in the intense heat as soon as emptied. The puckallies also leaked badly at first but, when coated with a compound invented by a transport officer, they seemed fairly watertight.

With thousands of men involved, some means of increasing the amount of water had to be found. The idea of digging for it in the desert is credited to Belliard, the French general who had brought 350 men to Cosseir from the Nile to build a fort and stop the flow of recruits from Arabia to the Mamalukes, the de facto rulers of Egypt. But Belliard's crossing had been relatively easy. His men had ridden on camels with 400 supply camels and an escort of 60 friendly Arabs, while his first diggings had been at Cosseir, which, up to then had been supplied with water from Arabia.

Realising that only by finding large quantities of water on the line of march could his men hope to reach the Nile, Baird ordered Murray to dig at any likely spot. Then, after a week's frenzied activity, Admiral Blankett appeared out of the blue with a letter from General Hutchinson, Abercromby's successor. The first message to arrive from the Mediterranean, it highlighted the problems that bedevilled the whole operation. While Blankett confirmed that sailing north was impossible, Hutchinson — obviously with no knowledge of seasonal conditions in the Red Sea — wrote that he was anxiously expecting Baird to reach Suez and join up there with the Turks while he remained near Cairo. Their combined forces could then march down the Nile to besiege Alexandria.

With this proof of Hutchinson's ignorance of his movements, Baird was about to send orders to Murray to push on to Keneh and open up communications down the Nile, when a Mamaluke arrived with a more recent letter from the General, informing him that all the country from Cairo to Alexandria was in British hands. The Mamalukes had come over to their side and General Coote* was encamped with 5,000 men before Alexandria, where Hutchinson was himself waiting for the Turks before besieging Cairo. While delighted at these successes, Baird and his staff were plagued with doubts as to whether the fighting would be over before they could get to Lower Egypt and all their efforts would have been in vain.

Although only half the route had been reconnoitred and while determined that no lives should be lost for want of taking every possible precaution, Baird decided that, if they were to see action, an attempt would have to be made on the desert crossing.

He divided his army into four divisions, Beresford with the 88th

*Nephew of Sir Eyre Coote

and some companies of sepoys to lead the advance. They were to march at night, making their first stop 10 miles from Cosseir where some water had been found. After rest and refreshments, they would continue another 10 miles to the half-way stage between Cosseir and Moilah. There they would halt for the day. The next day's march should take them to Moilah where they would find water and provisions. If the men were fatigued, they could remain there an extra day.

The orders for the march demonstrate Baird's understanding of what was then a novel concept of teamwork, with the chain of command extending from the top down to each individual soldier who had to assume personal responsibility for his own safety.

Advice to divisional commanders warned them to use their initiative in solving problems that might arise.

"Colonel Beresford," he wrote, "thinks the best mode of marching is 15 miles at night and 5 in the morning. I would recommend marching the whole distance without halting if you find your men not too fatigued." But on the vital matter of water rationing, his orders were specific.

> "You will not issue more than one gallon of water per man which may be given as soon as you arrive at your ground in the morning. But on no account is any to be issued on the march. The bags that leak must be emptied first and as your camp kettles will not be wanted for cooking, water may be started into them from the leaky bags while you wait."
>
> "Careful, steady men should be appointed in each division, and the principle should be explained to everybody."

Andrew Pearson says that the orders were considered oppressive by some of the men, particularly the one that completely banned the use of intoxicating drinks. But — "the main body of the men knew that the General in command was acting from personal experience, and the men strictly obeyed their instructions."*

Beresford's division set out on the evening of 21st June, with Baird accompanying it part of the way and when he returned to base everything seemed to be going to plan. The stopping place was reached on time. But on unloading the water bags from the camels they were found to have leaked so badly that some were completely empty. With the supply from the newly dug wells intended only for topping up, the horror of the situation for over 1,000 men was apparent.

Information was at once despatched to Cosseir, where Baird ordered the second division to delay its march and sent 50 camels

*Autobiography of Andrew Pearson. Republished by *Bullfinch* as THE SOLDIER WHO WALKED AWAY. (1987).

laden with water and another 50 to assist with possible casualties. He wrote to Beresford suggesting he send as many of the sick as the camels could carry on to Moilah and asked him to state his opinion, 'openly, fairly and fearlessly' as to whether he thought the march was still a practical proposition. If 'yes', he was to march on to Moilah, then send on parties to dig for water at any likely spots between there and Legeta before proceeding further. If 'no', he was to return at once to Cosseir.

Beresford's difficulties had meanwhile been increased by a new factor. The marches, planned on information by the Arabs, were found to be several miles longer than expected, so that more camels would be needed and these were in short supply. He nevertheless told Baird he would press on.

For two days the fate of the expedition lay in the balance. Then came news that Murray had found water at places 4 and 8 miles past Moilah. With the water bags repaired and re-proofed and the second division ready to move, an overall strategy began to take shape — though everything would depend on Beresford making it to Legeta. From there he would send forward two companies of the 88th to dig wells at intervals to the Nile. The second division was also told to dig at any likely spot. To make the most effective use of the water bags, the 88th, on reaching the stopping place before Keneh, sent back theirs to Legeta for the second division. In the same way, the second sent theirs back to Moilah for the third, and so on.

There are several accounts of the march.

Pearson says the 61st did not march in strict formation. The troops were told to break up into straggling parties with each man not more than three yards from a comrade. He says they must have looked more like wandering Arabs than soldiers. They suffered greatly from the heat. Yet orders were so strictly observed that the Regiment lost only one man. A drummer stole into the regimental doctor's tent and drank a dram of arrack. He dropped dead on the spot and his body 'instantly became black as coal'.

De Noe moved out from Cosseir with the second division at 4 in the afternoon and marched the 16 miles to the first springs by 2 in the morning. Some of the rear-guard who straggled were forced to increase their rate to catch up. The sun had risen and they arrived exhausted. One man died in de Noe's tent.

Another officer described the heat of the day as far greater than any of them had experienced in India. At times they found sleep impossible and the lack of it impaired their ability to march.

The paymaster, John Rider, who was 'naturally corpulent and, from a long habit of indulging himself, extremely indolent', had reluctantly accepted the post because it had been offered him as a favour. Being a civilian and not under military discipline, he decided to ride ahead of the troops on horseback. He managed quite well until the second day when he came up with the advance guard pitching their tents for the day. The C.O. of the party and the surgeon did their best to dissuade him, but he was determined to continue the journey. He rode on with his servant until 2 p.m., when he was suddenly taken ill. He lay on the scorching sand for two hours before he died. His servant tried to scrape a hole in the sand to bury him and managed, by the aid of a compass, to rejoin the army at 8 in the evening.*

On 27th June, the day Baird set for his departure from Cosseir, news of Wellesley's inability to sail at last arrived with a contingent under Colonel Champagne. The correspondence included the private letter already alluded to and a long Memorandum of advice on the expedition, which was now of little use. Baird's departure was thus delayed until 30th. Riding an Arab horse and accompanied by Auchmuty, he reached Moilah the following day. That the dangers and uncertainties of the crossing were still far from over is evident from a letter by Auchmuty to the officer left in charge at Cosseir.

> "We are certainly in a bad scrape. We can hardly go forward or back and the prospect does not brighten; but we must not despair. Among the causes of uneasiness is not hearing from Hutchinson. The General's plan is now to push forward everything on the road to Keneh, collect all the camels we can find (and I fear we shall not muster many), and send them back to Cosseir until we get a letter — we must then finally decide."

Arriving at Keneh on 5th, Baird found the troops had been well received by the natives who came to meet them with fruit, bread and pitchers of water for sale. At first the price charged for a small pitcher of water or a melon was a rupee: but as the Nile was approached the prices fell dramatically. The scene on their arrival at the river, wrote Pearson, "beggared description. As if an electric shock had passed through each of us, officers and men, alike burning with thirst, we rushed off to get a draught of water, with no respect for persons."

By sending the camels back to Cosseir, Baird had ensured the troops there could be brought up with the least delay; but he had cut off his own line of retreat and placed himself in a kind of no man's land. Day followed day with no reply from Hutchinson to the daily letters he had sent since he arrived at Cosseir. To keep up morale and

*Memoirs. William Hickey.

meet possible attack he took up defensive positions, commandeered all the boats he could for the journey down the Nile and continued to send off urgent letters.

Then on 27th, after three weeks at Keneh, came the long awaited news from Hutchinson. Dated 10th June, it showed again the problems of communication that had beset both commanders.

> "I have written to you frequently. I did not inform you of the surrender of Cairo because from your letters I concluded you were marching towards me ..... indeed, everything that related to you tended to embarrass me in a most extraordinary degree.
>
> "Before your arrival we had nothing but an unauthenticated rumour of a force from India, which Sir Ralph did not believe; consequently I could not have any idea of your force, or of the time you were likely to arrive. Your destination was a matter of which I had never heard, indeed, when you mentioned it in cypher, I was incapable of comprehending it as I do not possess the key — .
>
> "The conveyance of this country is often very tardy and frequently never reaches its destination at all. I have sometimes received the first, second and third copy at the same time and from the same messenger. Your last letter was three weeks on the road."

But now at least Baird's doubts about advancing were settled. He was informed that Hutchinson had an order from Lord Hobart, Secretary of State for War, that the sepoys were to be used for garrison duty at Alexandria. In addition, as General Menou, the French C-in-C, seemed determined to put up a stubborn defence of Alexandria, Baird's 'able assistance and cooperation' would be welcome and Hutchinson would await his arrival.

Baird at once began to push forward his troops down the Nile and ordered Colonel Montresor to bring his division from Cosseir. Thanks to the experience gained, with more camels, water and provisions and with the precise distance known (20 miles longer than at first estimated), the march was completed without loss.

A grand total of 7,886, of whom 4,127 were natives of India, including 666 'public and private followers', eventually made the crossing. The losses suffered by the army were just THREE men.

CHAPTER 12

Egypt. Garrison duty. The plague. The Mamalukes. 1801 — 1802.

It proved impossible to assemble enough boats to transport the army down the Nile. Those commandeered had to be used to carry the stores, the least fit men and the 30 guns dragged to Keneh by the few available bullocks. The rest of the troops had to walk.

The Nile was in flood and, with the irrigation canals to towns and villages full to overflowing, the troops were ordered to give the river a wide berth and, at the first sign of flooding, to make for high ground.

Baird embarked on 31st July. He reached Gizah, about 9 miles from the Pyramids, on 8th August and was gathering his troops at Rosetta to march on Alexandria when a letter arrived from Hutchinson with the shattering news that the French were about to surrender. For an army that had toiled across seas and desert and were now thirsting for action, no greater anticlimax could be imagined. Their only consolation, says Pearson, was that the French Commander, on hearing that the Indian Army under the generalship of Sir David Baird had arrived, decided that further resistance was useless..

Baird saw the rewards of his endeavours disappearing like a mirage in the desert crossing. He went to Hutchinson's HQ to find the surrender terms already settled. The French were to be shipped to France and, on orders from London, most of the British troops were to leave for Malta while the Indian Army remained in Egypt on garrison duty.

As commander of that Army he naturally expected to be in command and Hutchinson, who was in bad health and leaving for home, saw him as his logical successor. But on 18th came further orders from London; 6,000 of Hutchinson's men were to be combined with the Indian contingent, while the names of the generals to remain or be transferred to other commands were listed — all, that is, except Baird.

The Government that had ordered the expeditionary force to be sent from India was apparently ignorant of who commanded it and had sent no instructions on how he was to be employed. Could this have been connected with the fact that the orders had come from Lord Hobart, now Minister for War?

The officer ordered to remain in command of the garrison certainly thought so. Major-General John Moore, now meeting Baird for the first time, found that while he was to stay in Egypt, Craddock, an old school friend of Hobart, was detailed for active service in Italy. Incensed, he wrote: "this is a mode of acting that cannot fail to disgust officers who, though they have not been school-fellows of Lord Hobart, have been serving in every climate since the commencement of the war."

As Baird's career would later be closely linked with Moore's, the wording of this complaint is of particular interest in that it demonstrates a characteristic difference between the two. Unlike Moore's, Baird's protests are invariably confined to material facts and never personalized. When superseded by Wellesley, he refers to him as 'an inferior' officer and not as the Governor-General's brother. Similarly, when he later feels he has been denied rewards given to other officers, he never suggests that they are not entitled to them. This code of honour, from which he never deviated, partly explains the trust he inspired in those who served under him.

In the present instance, Moore found a way out by the excuse of a wound, for which Hutchinson gave him permission to return to England. The command of the Army fell to Lord Cavan who — it may be recalled — had, like Moore, a few days' seniority over Baird due to the inefficiency of Baird's agent. This was a matter of regret to Hutchinson, who wrote to Baird that if he had the power to alter it he would certainly do so. But the orders from England were specific and left him no discretion.

Apart from his relegation from an independent command, Baird foresaw problems in the amalgamation of the two armies. The sepoys and Indian servants had agreed to serve under officers who understood their culture and customs. To put them under the control of others who had had no regard for such details would destroy their morale. The pay of British regiments in India was based on their conditions of service and was higher than those on the Home establishment. It would be impossible to raise the pay of the whole army to theirs; yet to reduce Indian Army rates would cause real hardship. Indian officers were not allowed to employ soldiers as servants, but received an allowance to employ civilians. What was to happen to these people if the allowance was stopped?

Baird protested to Hutchinson and to the G.O.C. the Mediterranean on these matters. Hutchinson, not the most even-tempered of men, agreed on the difficulties but tried to smooth things over by suggesting that the British regiments would soon be sent to Europe, leaving only the Indians, and that even they would not be kept in Egypt for long.

To Baird's proposal that, as he was not mentioned in the orders, he should quit Egypt, Hutchinson said he could not allow it. The impulse to leave, as at Seringapatam, gives the measure of Baird's frustration. But whereas Harris would probably have been glad to have him out of the way, Hutchinson was too aware of his standing with the officers and men of the Indian Army to risk losing him. In the event he had no need to worry. Baird had become so involved with the day to day problems of those he commanded that he found it impossible to leave. After the amalgamation in November he wrote to Cavan:

> "Circumstances have so materially changed that I cannot think of deserting the army I brought from India."

Cavan, who seems to have had no great ambition for the command, was equally forthright:

> "I really confess I did not feel easy at the idea of your declining to act in any military command when the two armies were united. Your letter of yesterday entirely relieved me, and I am personally thankful to you for your expressions of readiness to assist me with your counsel and advice on all occasions to forward the service."

With the climate and lack of adequate supplies of food seriously affecting the men's health, Baird placed Dr McGrigor in charge of the medical department of the Indian Army. The choice was fortunate. McGrigor, who served in many lands in his long career, probably did more than any single man to improve the health of the common soldier. After his return to India he wrote an account of the expedition in which he says:

> "In no army perhaps, was the health of every soldier in it the care of every officer from the General downwards, than in the Indian Army. It would be doing violence to my feelings not to mention how much my duty was abridged by having such a Commanding Officer as General Baird. His military abilities are well known. His extreme attention to everything which regarded the health and comfort of the soldier, I must mention, was the principal cause of the great degree of health of the army."*

Soon after his appointment, McGrigor was in the hospital examining some men of the Bengal Regiment after they had been washing,

*Medical Sketches of the Expedition to Egypt from India. (1804).

when he discovered unmistakeable signs of the plague. His concern was increased by alarm lest he should have caught the disease himself. Quickly changing his clothes, he mounted his horse and rode in great agitation to break the news to Baird. He describes his reception:

> "At all times firm and less influenced by alarm than any man I ever met, General Baird was even less moved that I expected: perhaps on Dr White's opinion that plague was not a contagious disease, and who of late had had several interviews with Sir David on the subject.
>
> "He enjoined the greatest silence on me, but at the same time issued the necessary orders as to carrying into effect the precautionary means I had suggested to him on entering Lower Egypt, viz. those relating to the formation of pest houses, quarantines, observation grounds &c."

McGrigor had to remain in quarantine himself for three weeks and could take no active part in the proceedings. But, he says: "I believe that, after I made my report to Sir David Baird, I had not the least fear or alarm."[4]

Baird had meantime ordered the hospitals to be burned, which limited the loss of life to three sepoys. He then gave orders for whole streets of houses near the camp to be cleaned up by the army and for great quantities of rubbish to be burnt. Though much resented by the natives, this resulted in far fewer cases of the plague in the summer of 1802.

As usual, he did not confine himself to issuing orders. One officer observed:

> "When the plague suddenly appeared at El Hamed and many were struck with apprehension, Sir David was seen everywhere, animating and encouraging."

He was also concerned at another affliction that affected some of the men. Andrew Pearson was one of the many who went blind with ophthalmia. He says they had to move about in squads of 30, each hanging on to the coat-tail of the man in front, with one who could see a little in the lead. Baird had decided to send several of the sufferers home, when he got talking to a French medical officer who claimed he could restore the men's sight in three operations.

"In that case," said Baird, "if you can restore the sight of these men, I shall see you are handsomely rewarded."

The doctor replied that he was only too happy to perform the operations for the sake of humanity and wanted no reward.

See Appendix 4

Pearson, the first to be operated on, was held down by four strong men to keep him quite still while the doctor removed the cataracts from his eyes with a knife. He felt hardly any pain, but when the laudanum was applied the agony was so great that he broke away from the men. He soon fell asleep and woke to find all the pain had gone. The second operation hurt only a little and the third not at all. In this way hundreds of men had their sight restored.

To keep the men busy, Baird decided to send fatigue parties of 1,000 to the banks of the Nile, to remove Cleopatra's Needle for transporting to England. Wharves were built and a large ship had part of its stern cut away, ready to receive the Needle when it was brought down with the aid of wooden rollers. But, though the engineers had plans to get it on board, they were baffled by its size and weight. The men were ordered to take it back but, according to Pearson, this proved too much. They dragged it 100 yards from the wharf and left it there. Baird did not press the point. Knowing how the men must have felt, he decided to leave well alone. This abortive attempt to remove the 'Needle' by Baird was to have a curious sequel after his death.

Apart from its day to day problems, the Army soon became involved in a life and death struggle between the Turks and the Mamalukes. The latter were originally slaves imported into Egypt from Caucasia. In the 13th Century they had revolted and taken over the government of the Country. Though defeated in 1517 by the Turks when Egypt became part of the Ottoman Empire, their remoteness from the Central Power and the weakness of Turkish administration left them the de facto rulers, able to extort taxes from the peasants and not allow a piastre to enter the Turkish coffers.

For treachery and cruelty there was little to choose between them and the Turks. But they had given valuable assistance to the Indian Army and inspired respect for their courage. The Turks, however, saw the presence of their army in this distant part of their Empire as a godsent opportunity to exterminate their unruly subjects.

Baird's interest in the affair was two-fold. He was under an obligation to the Mamalukes for their help since his arrival at Keneh, and his return to India would probably be through territory controlled by them. In addition, he had made friends of some of the Beys (Mamaluke leaders), who looked upon him as their protector.

On the 6th October, he wrote from El Hamed to inform Hutchinson that the Beys had been invited to Alexandria by the Capidan Pasha (Commander of the Turkish Fleet) to be officially thanked for their help in the Allied cause. Some of the Beys had stopped en route to express their fears that, once in Turkish hands, their lives would be in danger. They wanted to remain at Rosetta until assured by Hutchinson they could proceed in safety.

Denying any wish to interfere in politics, Baird added: "nothing but the most earnest entreaties from Osman Bey Perdicci whom I in some measure regard as a personal friend could have induced me to address Your Excellency on this very delicate subject."

Hutchinson, who had already told Baird the Mamalukes should be supported, replied that the Beys had good reason for their fears and advised Baird to send an officer with them to show the Turks they were under British protection.

Next day Baird went to see the Beys at Rosetta, to explain Hutchinson's letter and to impress the Turks. On 11th he called again to introduce Colonel Montresor, with a party of 12 grenadiers and 20 dragoons to accompany the Beys, ostensibly to take charge of their horses. All seemed well until 15th, when some alarming news arrived from Montresor. The Capidan had sent the Beys a letter telling them it was unseemly to seek protection from Christians. If they came alone, 'by the Sultan and the Prophet no harm would befall them'. Against Montresor's advice, the Beys had gone into the Turkish camp unescorted.

That their fears had been well founded was shown a few days later. As they were rowed out to pay a ceremonial visit to a Turkish frigate, they were suddenly attacked by their escort and fired on by the frigate. Three Beys were killed and the rest imprisoned.

At Cairo, meanwhile, the Grand Vizier (Turkish C-in-C) was arresting some Beys and asking that those in the British camp at Gizah be handed over to him. Outraged at such treachery, Hutchinson wrote to the Grand Vizier:

> "I have just heard with the greatest astonishment that, notwithstanding your most sacred promises, you have caused the Beys to be arrested: that one of them has been assassinated and that others are your prisoners. You have left me the choice to avenge the assassination or to be an accomplice to it. There is not a moment to lose: I have just reinforced the Governor of Gizah, and General Baird is charged with the execution of my orders; be assured I will never retreat from them in the smallest degree ....."

He then sent the letter, open, to Baird for forwarding to Colonel Ramsay the Officer Commanding at Gizah, who was to deliver it in person. Having read it, Baird immediately sent it on to Ramsay and began to prepare for emergencies. Having already despatched the 86th Regiment to Gizah by water, he took control of all the boats in the area and ordered a gunboat manned by soldiers to be stationed on the River to search all down traffic for Mamalukes on board and to stop all Turkish boats up-stream. He also sent a detachment to Fort St Julien with instructions for the officer in charge to 'suggest' that, as the place was overcrowded, it would be best for the Turks to move out. With his small detachment of artillery installed, he informed the Pasha that no boats would be allowed up or down the River without passports.

Ramsay, at Gizah, playing for time until the 86th arrived, told the Grand Vizier he was indisposed but would deliver Hutchinson's letter as soon as possible. The Vizier seemed satisfied but said he had heard that General Baird had been directed to lead an armed force to Cairo to demand the Mamalukes' release. He strongly deprecated such a threat and asked Ramsay to tell General Baird he was prepared to discuss the matter with any authorised person. Middlemore, who accompanied Ramsay, later commented on the Vizier's reaction:

> "The Turks were more particularly alarmed when they heard that Sir John Hutchinson proposed to despatch General Baird against him; his character as a soldier, which they had many opportunities of studying, more effectively awed them into submission than anything else could have done."

When Ramsay finally delivered the letter, the Vizier said he did not believe a matter of such trifling importance as the Beys' release should endanger the English alliance with the Porte. The Beys were perfectly free to go but had said they were happy to stay. Being unable to dispute this, Ramsay withdrew. The Vizier next sent a letter to Baird by Rosetti, the Austrian Consul, accompanied by a high-ranking Turkish officer who assured him that the British Ambassador at Constantinople had agreed to the Turks having a free hand to deal with the Mamalukes as they saw fit.

After the interview, Rosetti, who was on friendly terms with the Mamalukes from having been used by Napoleon as an intermediary, told Baird that he was taking a letter to Hutchinson, signed by the Beys, asking his permission to allow them to go to Constantinople. But he added in confidence that it had been signed under compulsion and that the Beys still regarded themselves under British protection.

What Hutchinson's reaction to the letter would have been is impossible to say. The previous day he had handed over the Army and boarded ship for home, apparently without taking Cavan into his confidence and leaving no clue as to his intentions. In this extremity Cavan appealed to Baird for advice.

Repeating that his main aim was to ensure the safe return of the Indian Army via the Red Sea, Baird advised Cavan to send an able negotiator to the Vizier to settle matters amicably. He suggested that, as the Turks were determined to get the Beys out of Egypt, one possibility might be to secure a pension or sum of money for them to settle in some other country.

> "By this measure," he concluded, "the honour of the British may be saved and harmony restored between us and the Vizier. I need not add that, should it meet your Lordship's approbation, no time is to be lost in setting it on foot and none so proper as the present, immediately after your Lordship's assuming chief command."

His suggestion was adopted. Cavan sent Brigadier-General Stewart to Cairo with authority to arrange for the Beys' release in order to 'restore friendship and harmony between us'. A week later the Beys were set free to join their followers at Gizah, pending the arrival from Constantinople of Lord Elgin, who had been empowered by the British Government to negotiate between them and the Turks.

On 19th January 1802, Lord Elgin's Secretary, accompanied by Cavan, paid the Mamalukes a visit before going on to confer with the Grand Vizier. By 23rd there were strong rumours that a deal was about to be made handing them over to the Turks. Stewart, who had not been at the discussions, was so outraged that he sent word to Cavan that he felt duty bound to warn the Mamalukes of their danger.

The warning was unnecessary. Sensing betrayal, the Beys had already made plans for flight to Upper Egypt. As they moved with their followers from Gizah to set up camp near the Pyramids, 'all the garrison,' says de Noe, 'saw these brave fellows preparing to leave with great regret'.

On hearing of the flight, the Vizier asked for a British force to assist in pursuing them. But this Cavan refused.[5]

For Baird the outcome was satisfactory. He had secured the safe return of his Army to India, which took place in late Spring, following the Treaty of Amiens that brought an uneasy peace to war-weary France and Britain. The march to Suez took place in June, with the Army's strength down by 3,500. The 10th, 61st and 88th Regiments

See Appendix 5

were to sail for Europe, while the 7th Bombay Regiment had to remain in quarantine with a few cases of the plague. One notable casualty was Lachlan Macquarie, taken ill in May and almost 'bled to death' by the surgeon. His recovery, as he wrote later, was hastened by Baird's daily visits and he was able to cross the desert on a palanquin.

Before embarking at Suez, Baird wrote to Sir Home Popham, thanking him for his cooperation. His concluding paragraph was prophetic and unconsciously ironic.

> "Should it ever be my lot to be on active service on any future occasion where the army and navy may be required to act together, I can only add that it will be a source of real satisfaction again to cooperate with you and, if not, I shall wish it to be my good fortune to meet with an officer possessed of your zeal, ability and military experience."

Although the Indian Army had fought no battles, their trials and tribulations had developed a strong esprit de corps amongst officers and men. As de Noe confirms, this applied equally to the Sepoys who 'had a truly admirable sense of honour, and a wonderful desire to vie in self-control and bravery with the Europeans in dangerous situations'.

In popularity this marks the high point in Baird's career. De Noe, sailing for Europe with the 10th, writes:

> "We parted with regret. This admirable leader had been distinguished throughout by the keen interest he took in the officers under his command and by his concern for the common soldier."

Another officer wrote of Baird's "unremitting care for the troops, who daily witnessed his anxious attention to their wants and comforts — at the same time he enforced the most rigid discipline and gave the utmost protection to the natives whose confidence he gained."

In India the Army was greeted tumultuously at each Presidency in turn, receiving a singular honour in the form of medals struck and presented to every member of the force to mark the first occasion of Indian troops serving outside their own country.

Baird arrived with the Bengal contingent in Calcutta on 31st July, to a brilliant reception laid on by Mornington in his new Government House. Among the honours he received were the Colonelcies of the 54th Regiment and the Turkish Order of the Crescent, which allowed him to assume the title of Knighthood.

In England, the news of the Egyptian victory, coming after years of defeat and humiliation for the British Army, was received with rapture. And, by a strange quirk, the popular hero of the hour was one who had taken no active part in the campaign. The story of Baird's captivity and subsequent triumph at Seringapatam had already made his name familiar to ordinary people. This new adventure, in which he led his Army from India to Egypt, appeared to have all the mystery and romance of a tale from the Arabian Nights. Songs were composed in his honour and half-penny editions of his life with bad wood-cut illustrations were sold in the streets.

CHAPTER 13

Cape of Good Hope. Capture. 1805 — 1806.

After his return to Bengal, Baird was appointed Governor of Fort William. But, within a month, he obtained a transfer to Madras, where he was given command of a division. The move was a grave error of judgement. There would soon be a war against the Mahrattas in the North West Provinces as well as South India. Had he remained in Calcutta, Lord Lake, the new C-in-C, would undoubtedly have found him an important command in the field whereas in the South, Wellesley, now firmly established as the outstanding leader, was bound to play the dominant role.

Baird practised his usual principles of firm discipline and training for the battles ahead. But, for reasons not altogether clear, they failed to produce the expected response. On the march to Arcot he had difficulty in feeding his troops — not an unusual situation for commanders to find themselves in, – but after the smooth efficiency of the Egyptian expedition he was in no mood to accept it. He complained to the C-in-C that his camp followers were 'reduced literally to a state of starvation' while the Collector responsible for supplies remained in comfort fifty miles away.

The C.O.s of some regiments also failed to come up to his standards. The Artillery took four days to advance 28 miles then halted on the fifth, holding up the passage of the whole division through a pass in the Ghauts. Baird peremptorily ordered the C.O. to march.

The reasons for this slackness are uncertain, but Baird's efforts to instil discipline were not popular, in spite of his setting the pattern he expected others to follow. Allowing only a few hours for rest, he was fully occupied with his duties. After the day's march he visited every regiment and corps; then, reconnoitring the route for the next day he had an evening parade at which every regiment was inspected.

Aware that some regarded his attention to detail as unnecessary, he insisted there was no other way to keep up morale and discipline. 'The time will come,' he said, 'when they will be thankful to me for keeping them in order. They may grumble now, but they will forget all these little annoyances when they cross bayonets with the enemy.'

He was not destined to put his theories to the test. Soon after the River Tumbudra was reached, a large section of his division was drafted into that of his old rival, now Major-General Wellesley. It was obviously to be a repeat of the old story. He protested to the Madras Government but, getting no satisfaction, realised at last that he had reached the end of the line. He applied for leave and, in February 1803, embarked on the *True Briton* for home.

That his humiliation was largely self-inflicted can hardly be denied. He should have known that Mornington would not allow him again to stand in the way of his brother, who had now, in any case, given proof of his military genius. But the Madras Presidency, the scene of his early sufferings and ultimate triumph, held to the last a sentimental and fatal attraction.

Now, having quit forever the land where half his life had been spent, new adventures crowded in on him. The *True Briton*, struck by a hurricane as it approached the Cape, was driven deep into the South seas. It just managed to stay afloat and make its way to St. Helena, where news had arrived that England and France were again at war. Eager for action, Baird chartered a South Sea whaler for himself and his staff (which included his aide, George Middlemore, who was destined to return there 23 years later as Governor during Napoleon's last days of exile).

In the Bay of Biscay, the whaler was chased and captured by a French privateer. With all his worldly goods on the ship, Baird asked to remain on board. The French skipper agreed on condition he signed to say that he and his officers were prisoners of war and would take no action to delay the whaler. The prize set out for Bordeaux but, when food and water ran out, changed course for Corunna. They were sighted by a British man-of-war and the whaler again changed hands. Baird now boarded a cutter to the main fleet off Ushant and, reaching Falmouth safely, arrived in London to a hero's welcome.

In November 1803, he was exchanged for a French general and appointed to the Eastern District under Sir James Craig, a fellow Scot and an old friend from India. That he continued to harbour a sense of grievance is not surprising and some of his old cheerfulness was replaced by a degree of reserve. He was becoming even more set in his ways: stubbornly self-reliant and increasingly disillusioned with politicians.

"A fine soldier-like man, with such a determined air that you might draw the inference from his countenance that he was ready if ordered, to march into a fiery furnace", was how Fletcher Wilkie, a young officer remembered him.

After his long exile, adjustment to army life in Britain was not easy. Conditioned to the Indian climate and the customs of the Anglo-Indian Army, tainted by association with the get-rich-quick, wealth-flaunting Nabobs, the returning officer was not held in high regard by the Establishment. Even Wellington found this on his return. In a letter of advice to his friend John Malcolm, who came home in 1813, he wrote:

> "I have frequently been astonished at the indifference with which public men in England considered the talents of those who served in India — - — to hold office in England is a favour conferred upon the individual and he who has the disposal of the patronage of the Crown must be induced to bestow office by motives of friendship for the individual, by a sense that he can serve his interests, or is more eminently qualified than another to serve the public.
>
> "Although I had long been in habits of friendship with public men of the day, and had some professional claims to public notice, when I returned to England, I believe I should have been little known and should not be what I am, if I had not gone into Parliament — - -."

Baird was a Tory, but had no inclination to enter politics, having the good sense to realise, (like Sir John Moore who had a brief spell as MP early in his career), that his attitude to life unfitted him for the wheeling and dealing so essential for success as a politician. And though the Tories were in power, he was unlikely to receive patronage either from motives of friendship or for his readiness to serve the interests of a Member. He would certainly not have had the support of Hobart or Mornington when they were in the Government. So there remained only the chance of a situation where he was 'more eminently qualified than another to serve the public'. And it was precisely this that launched him on his next enterprise in the Summer of 1805.

The Cape of Good Hope, that vital link on the sea route to the East, had changed hands twice during the French Wars. Captured from the Dutch in 1786, it had been foolishly handed back at the Treaty of Amiens. Now, Lord Castlereagh, newly appointed Secretary for War in what would be Pitt's final administration, decided the Cape must be retaken.

His choice of Baird to command the invading force and Sir Home Popham as his naval support, was purely on practical grounds, for neither was popular with the Establishment. But both had an intimate knowledge of the Cape and its defences, while they had co-operated harmoniously in the only successful amphibious operation of the War, most others having ended in disaster due to lack of preparation, inter-service rivalry and the inefficiency of army commanders.

Castlereagh had been receiving secret reports from the Cape for some time. According to these, the Dutch Governor, General

Janssens, was a brave soldier but his resources were estimated at 1,500 regular troops, some burgher cavalry and a few hundred Hottentot infantry, while some Colonists were said to have remained well disposed to the British. Baird, who had been privy to the reports, was given instructions that were vague to the point of being contradictory.

He was to mount a surprise attack but was first to summon the Colony to surrender. Alternatively, he could open negotiations with the leaders (taking care not to waste too much time over them), grant favourable terms and take possession of the place 'with the least hazard to the ships and troops'. On capturing the Colony he was to take over as Lieutenant-Governor.

His army of about 7,000 would assemble at Cork. Drawn widely from the United Kingdom, it had one brigade composed of 71st, 72nd and 83rd, (the HLI, the Seaforths and the Argyles), another of the 24th, 38th and 83rd, (South Wales Borderers, South Staffs and the East Lancashires), with 211 dragoons, 300 artillery and 545 raw recruits.

Baird arrived to find that 500 men and several hospital staff had not shown up and there was a serious shortage of ammunition. On 2nd August he complained to Castlereagh, only to receive a reply that suggested he was prevaricating. After a month's threatening and cajoling, some of the ammunition had arrived and with the missing men — raw recruits of no value for the invasion — safely on board, he professed himself reasonably satisfied.

He was delighted to be in harness again with Popham and to have the support of Beresford, now a Brigadier-General. He had also been pulling the strings of patronage. Apart from his old Regiment, the 71st, his brother Joseph was in command of the 83rd while one of his aides, the Hon Alexander Gordon, was the third son of his sister Charlotte.

On 31st August, the fleet sailed quietly out of Cork and headed south. Its departure, kept secret as possible, would not in any case have roused much curiosity. The French were in camp at Boulogne and invasion scares were rife. The Navy had been blocking Cadiz for months and there was a feeling in the air that a great naval battle was imminent. Slipping past the squadrons off Cadiz awaiting the arrival of Nelson, the fleet anchored in Funchal harbour, Madeira, on 28th September. The frigate *Narcissus* with Captain Sorell, one of Baird's aides, on board, sailed on to St. Helena to find what information the Governor might have on the strength of the forces at the Cape.

The next port of call was to be Rio but, when two transports were wrecked off the Roccas, it was decided to put in at Salvador in Brazil. Relations between Baird and Popham remained cordial and they were united on a problem that bedevilled many amphibious operations. Captain Butterworth, the Naval Officer in charge of supplies, refused to consider himself under army authority, even where provisions for the troops were concerned.

From Salvador, Baird reported to Castlereagh:

> "Captain Butterworth, far from exerting himself to facilitate and expedite the service, appears to have thrown every obstacle in the way of it, and had it not been for the unremitting exertions of Sir Home Popham, our equipment must have been very considerably retarded both here and at Madeira."

As usual, he avoided personalising the problem by stressing that he had no desire to make a specific charge against Butterworth. He was bringing the matter to official notice 'that measures may be taken to prevent a future misunderstanding' and to ensure that a military commander on an amphibious expedition should have control over the provisions for his men.

Popham, who wrote to the Admiralty supporting Baird, also complained of defects in the transports which 'came out of England very ill-equipped, and to my great astonishment, had but a fortnight's bread on board'.

On another matter, Baird was showing diplomatic awareness. The dragoons were short of horses and Salvador provided the opportunity of acquiring some. He warned Captain Wilson, the cavalry officer in charge, that if the neutral Portuguese Government protested, he would have to disown sanctioning the purchase. Wilson obtained about 60 horses, but seems to have been an indifferent judge of horseflesh as they were found to be 'incapable of standing much fatigue' when put to the test.

The fleet sailed out of Salvador at the end of November, to arrive off Table Bay early on 4th January 1806. Nothing had been seen of the *Narcissus* (which was later found to have alerted the Colony when it chased a French frigate ashore). But another frigate had obtained information from a neutral vessel and, on the strength of this, it was decided to mount an immediate invasion.

The main fleet sailed for Robben Island, while the 24th Regiment was sent under escort to Camps Bay as a diversion. But now the elements staged their first distraction. The wind dropped and by the time the ships were at anchor between Robben Island and the Blue

Hills, it was afternoon; the attack had to be abandoned for the day. In the remaining hours of daylight, the Town's defences were reconnoitred, soundings taken and a cove 16 miles from Cape Town selected as the best landing place. Darkness fell with the weather set fair and seas calm.

By dawn the weather had again dramatically intervened. High winds whipped up the sea with huge breakers rolling up the beaches. Any attempt at landing was out of the question. The element of surprise gone, an alternative to waiting for the waves to subside had to be found. Saldanah Bay, 70 miles north, was known to be a secure landing place, though the move would have the disadvantages of a long march back to Cape Town over sandy ground in summer heat and under constant harassment from a mobile and resourceful enemy. But, faced with the prospect of days of inaction, Baird decided that Saldanah Bay it had to be.

On the night of 5th, the 38th Regiment and the dragoons sailed with some of the transports under the command of Beresford, while the main body prepared to sail the following day. But now the weather played another card. The 6th dawned with the waves surprisingly abated. And while the surf at the cove originally chosen was still too rough, the more sheltered Losperd's Bay looked a better prospect, although it was three miles further from the Town and the Blue Hills would have to be crossed.

An attempt at landing there having been decided on, 'a confined and intricate passage' was buoyed off by the Navy, a small transport was run ashore to form a breakwater and four ships were moored close in to cover the landing. First into the boats were the Highlanders and all went well at first. Then disaster struck. In the race to be first ashore, a freak wave crashed into one of the boats. It overturned and in spite of efforts by the sailors, 36 soldiers were drowned.

The landing went on apace and by the next morning 4,000 troops, a bare minimum of provisions and six naval guns drawn by sailors were ashore ready to move. There had been a few minor casualties from sharpshooters posted on the neighbouring heights, but these had been driven off and Baird directed his attention to the Blue Hills straddling the route to Cape Town, where the first serious resistance could be expected.

The march began at 4 a.m. As the van approached the Hills, mounted burghers could be seen moving along the ridges. Baird ordered his force into two parallel columns, the Highland Brigade on the left, the rest commanded by Colonel Baird in the absence of Beresford, on the right. The columns topped the ridge just as the enemy on

a. The troops attempted to land here on the 5th January, but the surf was too high.
b. Losperd's Bay, where the troops landed 6th of January.
c. The Marines of the squadron landed here with two field-pieces on the 8th January.
d. Where squadron obliged enemy to move encampment.
e. Where flag of truce came off.
N.B.—The figrues opposite Losperd's Bay show the position of the squadron when covering the landing of the troops—

1. *Diadem*	3. *Protector*
2. *Leda*	4. *Encounter.*

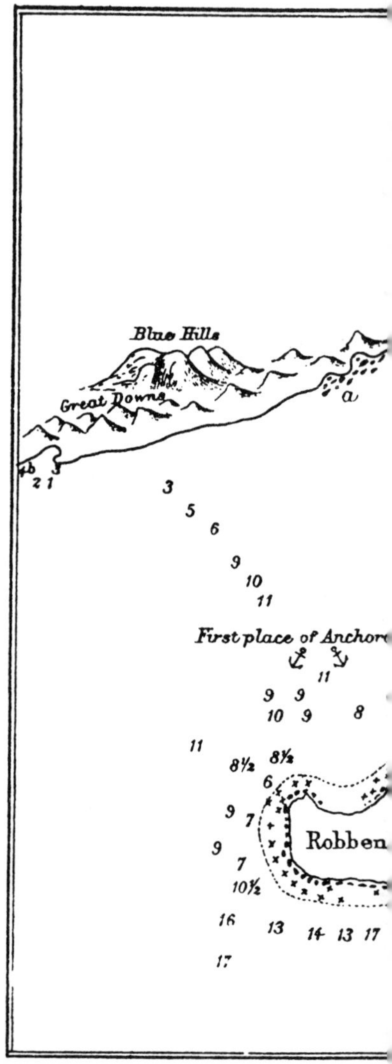

TABLE BAY WITH THE ROAD OF THE CAPE OF GOOD HOPE

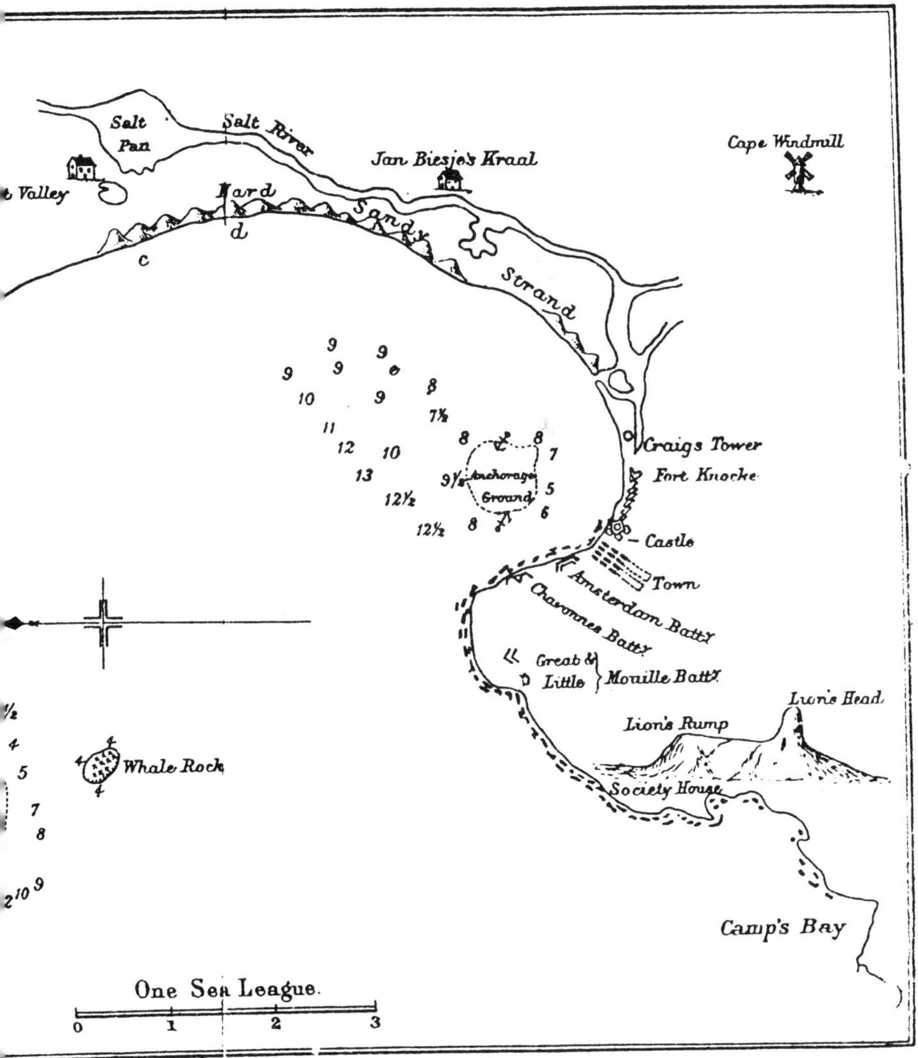

…hed to report of Commodore Sir Home Popham)

William Clowes & Son, Limited, London

the sandy plain below were forming a line of infantry supported by cavalry and sixteen cannon.

The columns were now deployed into lines and there was an exchange of artillery fire. As the first rounds fell near the enemy, some of their infantry were seen to break ranks and beat a retreat.

The burgher cavalry began to harass the right brigade but were held in check; at the same time the Highlanders advanced in the face of spasmodic cannon and musketry fire. For some unexplained reason they discharged their muskets prematurely, but as they continued to advance with the bayonet, more of the enemy took to their heels. Others retired in good order, their retreat covered by a company of mounted artillery.

Without cavalry, pursuit was impossible and Baird called a halt to count the losses. They amounted to 15 killed and 190 wounded. The enemy losses were evidently higher, though the exact number was never recorded. In spite of the easy victory, Baird's position remained critical. He was without a base and Janssen's guerilla army had still to be reckoned with. Allowing only a brief rest, he ordered the march to be resumed. The route lay over dry sand covered with shrubs and the men, enervated by long confinement on board ship, in clothing unsuited to the conditions of great heat, were soon in trouble. Many dropped from exhaustion while several of the sailors dragging the guns fell to the ground and died on the spot.

By the time the Reit Valley was reached, the need for water had become desperate. A search revealed only one small pool. The men frenzied with thirst, a complete breakdown in order loomed. It was averted by 'the commander-in-chief himself stepping in to superintend the distribution of the precious treasure'.*

Camp was set up in the open, while the Navy continued through the night to bring essential supplies ashore. Baird knew the Town's defences had been considerably reinforced during the British occupation and, with his few field guns, an assault could prove costly against determined defenders. Marching at dawn, he took up a position near the Salt River and had decided to have more guns brought ashore, when a flag of truce appeared on Craig's Tower. It was followed by an envoy from the Town Commandant, with a request for 48 hours to arrange capitulation terms. Baird gave him 36 and demanded possession of Fort Knocke. The Commandant accepted and, at 4 p.m. on 10th January, the terms dictated by Baird were signed.

All regular troops were to become prisoners of war and shipped to

*Wilson's own account.

Britain. Officers who had married into colonial families could remain on pledges of good behaviour; soldiers would be allowed to enlist into the British Army. Colonists who had taken up arms could return to their homes. Private property would be respected and all previous rights and privileges, including religion, would be respected.

All property of the Dutch Government must be surrendered and two Dutch ships, scuttled in the harbour, must be raised and given up to the British 'in a perfect state of repair'.

With the base he needed for action against Janssens and a safe anchorage for the fleet, Baird found himself faced with a pressing problem that had, in fact, hastened the Town's surrender. Only two days' supply of grain was in hand and, though the farmers had some wheat for delivery, the crop was light. A frigate was at once despatched to St. Helena for any available supplies and three transports to Madras for rice and wheat.

To establish a quick return to normality, Baird adopted a shrewd mixture of firmness and cajolery, leaving neither the Army nor the Colonists in doubt as to his intentions. One order to the Army went:

> "The interests of the expedition, the safety of the detached parties, as well as the articles of war, direct the kindest treatment of all the peaceful inhabitants. Violence against the person or plunder of their property, is immediate death without trial."

The proclamation to the Colonists on 11th January is typical. People in country districts were assured of British protection provided they stayed at home and went about their business. Those from in and around Cape Town serving with Janssens were warned that, if they did not return immediately to their homes, their property would be confiscated while anyone who went to join them could expect no mercy. All civil servants and those with official positions must take the oath of allegiance to the King at noon on the day of the proclamation. Willem van Ryneveld was appointed as Chief Civilian Magistrate, a post he had previously held under the British.

To bring Janssens to terms, Baird used the same strategy. The local militia was disarmed. All saddle horses were requisitioned for army use, paid for at a fixed rate and their owners were told they could reclaim them at the end of hostilities. Detachments of troops were sent to take possession of Simonstown, Muisenberg and Wynberg. On 13th, Beresford, back with his detachment, marched into Stellenbosch, about 20 miles from Cape Town, with three infantry regiments and some artillery, taking control of a large area of land which supplied Cape Town with food. He was given power to negotiate with Janssens and a letter from Baird to be presented at the right moment.

On hearing that Janssens was advising the farmers from the occupied area to return to their homes to avoid confiscation, Beresford decided to present the letter. As an example of the art of gentle persuasion it could hardly be bettered:

"Sir,

You have discharged your duty to your country as became a brave man at the head of a gallant but feeble army. I know how to respect the high qualities of such a man; and do not doubt that the humanity which ever characterises an intrepid soldier, will now operate in your breast to check the fatal consequences of a fruitless contest — - -."

The British forces that now hold the seat of government, the letter continued, were so strong that all Janssens could hope for was a temporary resistance which would result in the devastation of the country. Such a catastrophe could "never be contemplated without anguish by a generous mind, or be gratifying to the man who feels for the prosperity and tranquillity of the colony lately subject to his administration".

But if Janssens was determined to oppose so superior a force, bringing misery and ruin on the industrious and peaceful settlers, he (Baird) would feel his conscience clear and Janssens would have to justify his conduct to himself and his countrymen for "the further effusion of blood and the desolation of the country".

The letter concluded: "I shall not enlarge on your power of causing mischief to all its inhabitants; but persuade myself that the considerations of a more laudable nature will influence your decision and that you will manifest an immediate disposition to promote a general tranquillity.

"I have the honour to subscribe myself,
With sentiments of the highest consideration,
Sir, Yours, etc.,
D. BAIRD."

Finding Janssens softened up but still holding out for better terms, Baird ordered the 83rd to sail for Mosell Bay to cut off the enemy's retreat and joined Beresford to take charge of negotiations. In a last desperate throw, Janssens sent a modified draft of the terms which Baird firmly rejected and on 18th January, Janssens capitulated.

Admitting that the Dutch General must eventually have surrendered, Baird's achievement has received scant praise from most military historians. Fortescue, in particular, makes little of it and chides Baird for allowing the Scottish Regiments to take most of the glory. Perhaps the British tendency to dwell on disasters and retreats leads us to forget that taking the Cape was the most significant military success of the time. And, as J.W. Cole comments:

"The measures that Baird adopted were bold and skilful and the result is not to be undervalued because it was cheaply won."*

Janssens' army must have been one of the most diverse ever assembled. It included 400 mercenaries (Waldecks), half a battalion of Dutch regulars, 130 dragoons, 230 mounted burghers, 210 Dutch and Javanese artillerymen, 240 French sailors, 180 Hottentot infantrymen and 100 slaves.

The weakest element in this motley array had been the mercenaries. The name Waldecks is deceptive, as they were made up of Austrians and Hungarians who had been sold to the Dutch and had no desire to get themselves killed in a hopeless cause. When the first shots were fired, some of them had fled although, as Janssens verified, the rest of the army behaved well and retreated in good order. After the battle, he ordered the Waldecks back to Cape Town as unfit to associate with honourable soldiers and on arrival some of the officers committed suicide from shame. After taking the Town, Baird confined the Waldecks in a fort.

The capitulation terms were generous. The Dutch troops were repatriated to Holland on the understanding they took no part in hostilities against the British before arriving home. They could retain their private property, but all cavalry horses, arms and public property must be surrendered.

Baird and Janssens were soon on friendly terms. When Janssens sailed for Holland on 6th March, he sent Baird a private letter recommending the inhabitants to his protection:

> "They have their faults, but these are more than compensated for by good qualities. Through lenity, through marks of affection and benevolence, they may be conducted to any good."

How far Baird put these sentiments into practice will be seen. But first he had to stamp his authority on military and civilian. Desertion from the army was a continual problem at the Cape. The chance of disappearing into the outback to start a new life was a temptation that even the better type of soldier found it hard to resist. When the British had last evacuated the Colony, there had been a number of desertions. Baird now declared an amnesty for these men. Yet, far from solving the problem, his lenity may have made matters worse. Most of the Waldecks had taken up the offer to enlist in the Army rather than return to Europe and, not surprisingly, their loyalty to

*Memoirs of British Generals during the Peninsular War. Vol I (1856).

their new masters proved no stronger than to the Dutch.

Some deserted, were captured and flogged and a warning was given that future deserters would be even more severely punished. A few weeks later, courts-martial passed sentences of death on three at Simonstown and three at Cape Town. Many in the army believed the sentences would not be carried out — they were. The six were shot the same day. There were no more desertions.

Aware from experience that an army of occupation could soon get out of control, Baird took no chances. His methods, based on the maxim that Satan finds work for idle hands, was not to the liking of Fletcher Wilkie, one of the young officers. From 5 in the morning to 6 at night, he says, their days were filled with marching, guard-mounting, regimental parades, courts-martial, etc., but what really upset him was that officers had to parade with the men.

They were ridiculed by the Dutch who reproached themselves for having been defeated by a set of recruits.

"You see," they said, "even the officers are sent to drill."

After they became proficient at drill, field days began and fatigue parties were sent to erect batteries in case of invasion. Except for occasional Sundays off, says Wilkie, there was no leave to be had — although, on his own admission, he managed to see a good deal of the surrounding countryside.*

As news of the great Naval Victory at Trafalgar had not yet arrived, both Baird and Popham were concerned at a possible counter-attack by the French. In February, believing the Cape was still in Dutch hands, a French frigate took refuge in Table Bay. Below decks were 200 British troops taken off a transport in the English Channel and on their way to captivity in Mauritius. To their amazement, these men suddenly found themselves free. This was followed by rumours, false as it turned out, of the imminent arrival of a large French fleet. According to Wilkie, "a goose of a Dutchman came in and said he had seen a squadron of French at anchor in Saldanah Bay". After cavalry and artillery were despatched to the spot, the man confessed it was a hoax and said he was sorry.

Wilkie was amused. Baird was not. On 10th March he issued a proclamation that some ill-advised and malicious persons had been spreading false reports of the arrival of an enemy fleet. One such "was even wicked enough to state, in my presence, that he had not only seen an enemy fleet but had spoken to some of the officers at Saldanah Bay and had come to report the fact". As a warning to others,

*Fletcher Wilkie. Recollections of the British Army in the Early Campaigns of the Revolutionary Wars. (United Services Journal. 1836).

"Cornelis Maas is to be flogged round the town in the most public and exemplary manner tomorrow at noon by the Public Executioner, and will afterwards be transported out of the Colony."

Like many of his 18th Century contemporaries, Baird's conduct sometimes verged on the eccentric. As Wilkie observed, he looked at things with a different eye from other people. To prove his point he gave the following.

When news of Trafalgar finally arrived there was great rejoicing. The band on duty in the garden of the Governor's house, in an excess of enthusiasm, marched up to the window where Baird and Janssens were conversing and started to play a loud patriotic tune. They were ordered to stop and sent, bandmaster and all, to the guard-room for insulting a fallen enemy.

CHAPTER 14

Cape of Good Hope. Governorship and Recall. 1806 — 1807.

Baird has generally been regarded as having no ability as an administrator. This is surprising in view of the impressive list of reforms he introduced in his short time as Governor at the Cape.

There had been a shortage of grain before the British arrived. Now, with increased numbers, the threat of starvation loomed. Having sent to Madras and St. Helena for emergency supplies, Baird suspended the laws that had restricted the import of grain and offered a bounty until consignments arrived from North America. But fluctuating shortages had been chronic for years. With almost limitless agricultural land and a small population, a season of glut had been regularly followed by one of scarcity. The Dutch had appointed a Grain Commission to fix prices and compel farmers to bring in their corn to public granaries at below market price. But rather than incur the expense of the long haul to Cape Town, many farmers had fed their grain to their animals.

Baird rescinded all these regulations and appointed a Commission to fix two prices: one guaranteed to the farmer, the other for grain released from Government stocks to the public. Outside this a free market would operate with all duties temporarily removed from imported grain. The farmer was thus assured of a fair price and, by the release of Government grain, the public was protected from exorbitant prices in the open market. By November the shortage was over and the Commission wound up. The farmers continued to operate a free market while the public were safeguarded by the Colonial Granary, where surpluses were bought at a fair price and stored for emergencies.

The administration and the commercial and social life of the Colony had been restricted by a lack of regular communication. Baird decided to introduce a postal service. In February, he instructed all district magistrates that postmen (Hottentots of known integrity) were to be paid regularly. In March, he established a daily post between Cape Town and Simonstown. In May, he appointed a Postmaster General and issued regulations governing overseas mail and its distribution to country districts. By September, a General Post was established throughout the Colony.

He introduced many measures to improve public health, the need for which may be gathered from a single statistic in the *Gazette*. Out of 32 deaths, 30 were children aged 5 years or less.

In March he issued regulations for cleaning up Cape Town and imposed penalties for certain offences. Not satisfied with the results, a few months later he levied a tax on the townspeople, to have the work done more effectively. He introduced vaccination for smallpox, pointing out its effectiveness but adding there would be no compulsion on any families 'not anxious to submit to the operation'. Aware of the contagion brought by ships, he ordered health inspectors to board all incoming vessels and empowered them to impose penalties.

These and other changes gave widespread satisfaction to the Colonists and were praised by visitors, which included two famous sailors of contrasting characters and differing reputations – Francis Beaumont, the Hydrographer and William Bligh, of *Bounty* fame, on his way to take up his ill-fated appointment as Governor of New South Wales. Both wrote letters praising Baird and expressing their admiration for the peace and prosperity he had brought to the Colony.

So, it seemed, the success he had striven for was at last firmly within Baird's grasp. But, inevitably, Fate was preparing a bolt to deliver. He and Popham had carried out two successful operations, with none of the inter-service rivalry that had marred so many others in the War. Now, the Colony safe and Baird happily governing it, Popham's restless mind turned to new adventures. And, as luck would have it, there was one ready to hand.

The Spanish possessions in South America had for some time attracted the attention of military and naval commanders. In 1797, Sir Ralph Abercromby had written from the West Indies to Henry Dundas advocating the 'liberation' of the South American Colonies. He had suggested two expeditions, one from Barbados against Venezuela, the other from England via the Cape of Good Hope to the River Plate. Not long before leaving for the Cape, Popham had raised the same propositions with Pitt and Dundas. He set down his ideas and though tempted, the politicians had rejected them on the grounds of expediency. They did not want to offend Spain.

Now, kicking his heels at the Cape, Popham saw himself as a buccaneer in the Elizabethan style. He had the ships and the crews. All he needed was military support and for this he had to get the help of his friend Baird. His arguments ran thus.

The Cape was securely in British hands. After Trafalgar there was no danger of a naval attack. His ships were no longer needed to defend the place. The South Americans would welcome him as a liberator. He told Baird of his discussions with Pitt and Dundas. But instead of stating they had turned his plan down, he implied they were waiting for the right moment to put it into operation. The time had arrived. He was at the very spot from which the expedition was intended to be launched. Such an opportunity might never arise again. All he wanted was one regiment. He was going to make the attempt with or without it. If he failed through lack of military support, the responsibility would lie with Baird.

Baird was not convinced. He wrote privately to Colonel Gordon, Secretary to the Duke of York, that Popham was pressing him hard 'to make a dash for Buenos Aires (Reo de la Plata)', and he was aware of the great advantages to England from its capture. But he could not detach so large a force as a regiment without first knowing the state of Europe. If he could get the Hottentot Corps 'into some order' in a month or so and the Colony remained in its present tranquil state, he might reconsider the matter. Meanwhile another voice was added to Popham's. Beresford began to press his claim to command the expeditionary troops. After much deliberation, Baird detached his old Regiment, 71st, with a few artillery and with Beresford in charge, to sail with Popham. He also allowed his nephew, Alexander Gordon, to go and pick up what glory was to be had.

He informed Castlereagh and Colonel Gordon of his decision and gave his reasons, though his letters have a noticeable difference from the one sent privately to Gordon. He made no reference to being pressed by Popham:

> "I am aware I have taken upon myself a high responsibility, but the importance of the object in a national point of view, will, I trust, bear me out and ensure the approbation of his Majesty and his Royal Highness, the Commander-in-chief."

Of support from the Duke of York, he could rest assured. The Duke had few efficient generals at his disposal and had sympathy for Baird in his misfortunes. But unfortunately for Baird, his fate lay, not with the Duke or even Castlereagh but with a politician of a different calibre.

In January 1806 William Pitt had died and his administration was replaced by what came to be known, ironically, as 'The Government of All the Talents'. On 5th February, Castlereagh had handed over his office to William Windham, the gentleman and scholar whose brilliant conversation had captivated the aging Dr. Johnson. In opposition, Windham had produced bright ideas on military matters in speeches full of classical allusions. But in office he was indolent and completely failed to come to grips with the huge problems of administration involved in the war effort.*

But, though inept, he had the power to reverse the policies of the previous administration. When news of the capture of Cape Town reached England on 28th February, *The Times* gave a full account. The public and the City, long starved of good news on the military front, went wild with joy. 'The church bells were ringing', wrote Charles Lamb. In contrast, the Government remained strangely muted. Asked by a Tory if a vote of thanks was to be conferred on the Military and Naval Commanders, a Government spokesman replied that as the operations were not yet complete, a recommendation would be premature.

On 15th April when news of Janssens' capitulation arrived the matter was again raised. A Member of the Opposition asked if it was intended 'to confer any mark of approbation on those who had achieved the important conquest', and pointed out that this had just been done in the case of Sir John Duckworth, who had received a Vote of Thanks and a pension of £1,000 for forcing some French ships to surrender in the West Indies. Windham replied that the Government

> 'had not abstained from any want of approbation of the conduct of the officers and men who had been engaged in the operation. But the capture of the Cape was not a military exploit of that splendid nature that called for such a distinguished mark of approbation as the Thanks of the House, which should not be made cheap by being too frequently conferred — - -.

As an example of damning with faint praise, this would be hard to better. But the Government's partisanship is best illustrated by the rewards that had been given to the leaders of the capture of the Cape in 1795. Meeting less resistance than Baird (4 killed and 60 wounded), the leaders, Generals Alured Clarke and James Craig had received the KB while the Naval Commander, Sir George Elphinstone, had been made a baron (Lord Keith).

Baird's first intimation of the change of Government reached him in Windham's bare acknowledgement of his despatches on the fall of Cape Town.

> "It would have been more gratifying to His Majesty's feelings to have obtained possession of the Cape without the infusion of blood, but from the resistance you describe His Majesty feels great satisfaction in

*See *Peninsular Preparations* by Richard Glover.

> observing that the loss in killed and wounded was not so considerable as might be apprehended — -. The measures which you have pursued after the capitulation of Cape Town appear to have been perfectly judicious — -."

This reached Baird at the end of May. In mid-June, the Government received its first report of the South American expedition in a despatch from Popham en route from St. Helena and was at once thrown into a dilemma. It strongly disapproved of Popham both as an individual and a Tory. His high-handed action offended all their avowed pacific and liberal views. But what if he should capture the South American Colony? Could they afford to reject the spoils? They decided to wait and see.

So for Popham there was a conditional reprieve. Not so his reluctant accomplice. By lending his support, Baird had given Windham the pretext he required. On 26th July he wrote:

> "It is impossible a proceeding so extraordinary as that of detaching a considerable force on one service destined by His Majesty's Government for another without sanction or authority, either direct or implied, can meet with the Royal approbation, particularly as the measure is not justified on the grounds of necessity."

Baird was to consider himself recalled and to hand over the government to either Lord Caledon (a Whig MP), or to Major-General George Grey (brother of Lord Howick), the Lieutenant-Governor, whoever arrived first.*

Of this Baird would remain in ignorance for many months. But he had received news that Buenos Aires was in British hands and that Beresford needed reinforcements. He had hesitated before giving Popham his support, but now the die was cast he immediately despatched the 47th Regiment to the River Plate.

His prompt action was in sharp contrast with the hesitancy of the Government at home. When news of the expedition's success reached London in September, it was received with extravagant delight. There were scenes of jubilation in the streets as a conveyance with an escort of Jack Tars (who stopped occasionally for suitable refreshment) proceeded to the Bank of England to deposit a million dollars and a box of precious jewels, looted from Buenos Aires.

The Government was accepting the spoils but showed little public reaction. Their principles would not have allowed them to order the

*Caledon, an Irish Peer, was a Whig MP. Grey was brother of Lord Howick, the First Lord of the Admiralty.

conquest but, presented with the fait accompli, they lacked the nerve to denounce it. Instead, on 16th September, they issued Orders in Council regulating trade with Buenos Aires — though on the important matter of sending reinforcements to Beresford there was nothing but rumours. At last, at the end of October, came a remarkable *volte face*. Two expeditions were to sail. One, under Sir Samuel Auchmuty with an escort commanded by Admiral Stirling, would make for Buenos Aires. Sailing with it would be General Grey, Baird's replacement with the letter recalling him.

The other, a crazy brainchild of Windham, was a plan to send his protege and supporter in the House, Brigadier-General Craufurd, half round the world with 4,000 men to take Valparaiso. He was then to contact Beresford and, by a chain of forts, or some other method, establish 'uninterrupted communication, both military and commercial, between Chile and Buenos Aires'. He was to impress on the people of Chile that he had not come as a Conqueror, but to bring them British protection against the Spanish oppressors — just as Beresford had done at Buenos Aires.*

Beresford! Protection! If only Windham could have seen that begetter of liberty at the moment he was issuing his instructions. When Auchmuty and Stirling arrived at the mouth of the River Plate early in December, they were met by Popham and his fleet. Buenos Aires was no longer in British hands. The citizens, urged on by their priests and organised by a French emigré named Liniers, had mounted a sudden attack on the small British force in their midst and, after a brief and bloody contest, Beresford had been forced to surrender. He and his men were now prisoners of war.

There followed a vitriolic war of words between Stirling and Popham. But, as shown in a letter to Baird, Popham remained as perky as ever.

> "Here I am, once more a private gentleman in South America. I am superseded by Admiral Stirling. He has refused me a ship to go to England; he has now declared he will force me to go by the *Sampson* via the Cape and St. Helena."

Quoting Magna Carta, he said, this he was determined not to do.

He must have got his way for he did not travel to the Cape. The *Sampson* sailed into Table Bay on 15th January 1807 with General Grey, the new Lieutenant-Governor, aboard. The following day he stepped ashore.

*Craufurd's force ended up fighting at Beunos Aires.

Baird, though expecting some mark of disapproval now that Popham's venture had failed, had not yet received any intimation that he was to be recalled, although the letter was dated six months earlier. It was now presented to him by General Grey.

The hand-over was made as speedily as possible and on 17th, Baird, anxious to return home, came up against another example of the pettiness of the Government. He was hoping to travel on the *Sampson* and Captain Cummings, the Commander, said he would have been happy to accommodate him had he not been given positive orders not to remain at the Cape for more than 24 hours. He produced the orders, which were 'peremptory', for Baird to see.

Much to the astonishment of the Army and the people of Cape Town, Baird embarked the next day on the *Paragon*, a transport vessel. He was escorted to the water's edge by all the leading citizens, representatives of the Army and throngs of ordinary people.

Before leaving he had been presented with addresses from both the Dutch and English sections of the community. The first, signed by 49 representatives of the Court of Justice, the Burgher Senate and all Civil and Ecclesiastical Boards, expressed their deepest regret at his departure and begged him to accept their most grateful thanks for the paternal protection they had experienced under his administration.

> "By your wise and well-directed measures for our government, together with the unparalleled discipline of the troops under your command, our rights have been guarded and the whole Colony enjoys at this moment a state of tranquillity and plenty, seldom if ever equalled."

From the British residents an address in similar vein contained the following:

> "We feel ourselves highly gratified in having it in our power to congratulate your Excellency on our having witnessed, under your command, a discipline and good order in the Army never experienced before in this Colony; from the wisdom, justice and moderation of your civil government, you have the singular satisfaction of a Conqueror leaving the Conquered, beloved and regretted by them."

These addresses and other testimonials, together with private letters from outlying districts which were forwarded to him in England, were the only rewards Baird received for his services at the Cape. There is no reason to doubt that the sentiments they expressed truly reflected his achievements. On 19th February, Grey reported to Windham:

> "I have not made any change whatever in my predecessor's regulations, which appear to have given universal satisfaction and are, as nearly as possible conformable with those established by Earl Macartney in the year 1796."

Grey's report was not read by Windham. By the time it reached London, the 'Ministry of All the Talents' had fallen and Castlereagh was again War Minister. Not that this freed Baird from the stream of vindictive criticism that Windham had directed at almost every regulation he had issued.

In order to bring life back to normal as soon as possible, he had appointed some temporary civil servants. Windham regarded this as an infringement of his own powers of patronage and questioned Baird's right to do so. In reply, Baird could only state the obvious: that without them Government could not function. After the return to British rule, several people were owed money by the Dutch. Baird regarded this as unfair and appointed a commission to decide on their claims. Those found to be reasonable were paid by the Government. Here again, Windham decided he had exceeded his authority.

But the issue that brought the fiercest criticism was that of the Prize Money, although Baird had followed exactly the precedent set after the invasion of 1795. Derived from the sale of the Batavian Government's assets and the enemy shipping captured in Table Bay, the sum amounted to more than £300,000. Baird had ordered the sale of the goods and the proceeds remained in the hands of the Prize Agents until 25th April, when he was presented with a petition by the Burgher Senate bringing to his notice the serious effects of keeping so large a part of the currency out of circulation. The Colony had nothing to export. Everything had to be paid for in cash. They begged that the Prize Money be distributed to the captors and so released into circulation. Baird made no move until 1st June, when he received another petition drawing his attention to the inability of some merchants to pay their bills or make purchases. He then ordered the distribution of the Prize Money and wrote to Windham giving his reasons. Windham replied that he had again exceeded his authority.

> "It appears to His Majesty's Ministers to be somewhat singular that you should have acted thus promptly upon the opinion of the Burgher Senate, and still more so that you should have expected the proceedings adopted by you to be approved of; the Burgher Senate could hardly be considered disinterested in the opinion which they gave, though it was one which left them free from the Serious Responsibility attending the adoption of it."

The letter did not reach the Cape before Baird left, but its accusations had to be looked into by Castlereagh. Baird explained that, in ordering the sale of the goods, he had followed the precedent set by the previous British occupation. Some goods were perishable and others indispensable to the Services whose 'resources and comforts had been exhausted by the long voyage'. Many of the Colony's inhabitants were in great need and only by releasing the goods could they be relieved. To have allowed the money to accumulate in the hands of the Prize Agents would have been ruinous to the merchants and others. He had ordered an inventory of all the goods sold to be sent to England and, if necessary, the items could be checked and decided on again.

Castlereagh found these explanations satisfactory and there officially the matter ended.

Baird was received kindly by the Duke of York, who told him he entirely approved his conduct at the Cape and had only ordered his recall on instructions from the Government. This was some consolation, but his mortification, repeating the pattern of ill-luck that seemed to have dogged him through life, left wounds that were slow to heal. The effect was to further the retreat within himself that had been marked after his return from India. He had always steered his own course, looking at events and decisions from predetermined standards of his own. At the age of 50 he was not likely to change. With his faith in politicians still further shaken, his own principles would more than ever serve as the touchstone.

Nothing could have been more unfortunate than the timing of his term as Governor at the Cape, coinciding as it did with the period of office of the Ministry of All the Talents. And while he certainly presented Windham with an excuse for recalling him when he gave his support to Popham's wild venture (which would have been given by nine out of ten generals), such was the frenetic virulence of party politics at the time, the change of Government made his humiliation inevitable.

CHAPTER 15

Spain. To Corunna. 1808.

In August 1807, Baird commanded a division in the army under Lord Cathcart sent to capture the Danish fleet. He took part in the Siege of Copenhagen, where his old rival Wellesley distinguished himself in command of a brigade. Popham, who had been court-martialled and reprimanded for his attack on Buenos Aires, was also there co-ordinating naval and military operations with his usual energy.*

Soon after the siege, Lachlan Macquarie sailed in from a diplomatic mission to Russia. So tardy were communications that he believed Baird was still at the Cape. Hearing his friend had been twice wounded, he hurried ashore to be welcomed 'affectionately'. Baird's wounds turned out to be a broken finger and an injury to his collar bone: the ball having dropped into his tunic. He retrieved it and, finding it flattened, handed it to his nephew as a souvenir.

Returning to England in October, he spent the winter quietly until April, when he was appointed to command a Summer Camp for training regulars and the militia at the Curragh of Kildare near Dublin. About the same time, Castlereagh was setting up two military operations, though Baird does not seem to have been pressing for an active command, and it was by a strange catenation of events that he was drawn into his last great adventure.

Early in the Summer of 1808, reports were received from Spain of widespread resistance by Spanish patriots to Napoleon's armies of occupation. A popular rising in Madrid had been ruthlessly crushed. But others had followed at Valencia, the Asturias and Andalusia. In London, the news was hailed as the spark that would set Europe in flames and destroy the Napoleonic tyranny. Spain was transformed almost overnight from enemy to ally. Wellesley, about to lead an expedition to Venezuela, was directed instead to Portugal where the spirit of revolt had spread.

The Government seemed determined to take full advantage of the new turn of events. Yet, in private, its Ministers were grappling with a problem as to how this could be best achieved. Though Wellesley had sailed to the Iberian Peninsula and they believed him to be the right man for the command, the appointment of so junior a lieutenant-general was bound to rouse strong opposition. To most Whigs the name Wellesley was anathema while, at the Horse Guards, the

*Wellesley and Popham were in the three-man delegation sent to arrange the handing over of the Danish fleet.

SIR JOHN MOORE

Duke of York, determined to break the stranglehold of Patronage on Military appointments, was adopting the alternative evil of seniority.

The Government might have backed its choice and damned the consequences had there been no obvious rival to Wellesley. But there was. In a few weeks Sir John Moore, the darling of the Whigs, would be back from an ill-fated mission to the Baltic, where he had been sent to support the Swedish resistance to Napoleon.

In battle, Moore had proved himself a model of cool-headedness, but in diplomacy his conduct had been less than restrained. He had openly criticised Government decisions and had disagreed violently with Government officials. On different occasions he had been provoked to anger, to incoherence and even to tears. He had been recalled in disgrace from Corsica in 1795 after a quarrel with the Viceroy and had left Sicily in 1807 following a row with the envoy to Naples. On all these occasions he had been morally in the right, but had acquired a reputation for excitability and lack of judgement.

That the Government should hesitate to stake their reputation on such a general is understandable. They accordingly thought up an apparently watertight solution. Soon after Wellesley sailed for Portugal, they appointed two elderly guards officers, Sir Huw Dalrymple and Sir Harry Burrard, as first and second in command of the expeditionary force. Moore, daily expected from Sweden, would be told to sail on to Spain as third in the chain of command with Wellesley as fourth. Their hope was that Moore would be so annoyed at his exclusion from the supreme command that he would refuse to sail and so the practical direction of affairs would be left to Wellesley.

Annoyed Moore certainly was. But, sensing the trap and unable to resist the prospect of active service, he kept his head. He set out for Portugal on 31st July with his army from Sweden and firing a parting shot at Castlereagh that has a ring about it of Baird's protest at being superseded in India.

> "His Majesty's ministers have the right to employ what officers they please — - — but I have a right, in common with all officers who have served zealously and well, to expect to be treated with attention, and when employment is offered me, that some regard should be had to my former service."

Wellesley had preceded him by a mere 19 days. But those days were to prove decisive in the careers of both. On 21st August, the French under General Junot advanced on the British lines at Vimiero and, for the first time in the war in Europe, were forced to retreat. Wellesley, who was directing operations, requested Sir Harry Burrard's permission to advance and turn the retreat into a rout. Burrard refused and was supported next day by Dalrymple. The French came to discuss surrender terms. It was agreed they should be transported home in British ships with all their possessions.

When these conditions, enshrined in The Convention of Cintra, reached England, the euphoria evoked by the Victory at Vimiero was turned to anger and frustration, with the three Commanders recalled to answer for their actions to a Board of Generals. Wellesley, whose only guilt had been to sign the Convention, rode out the storm with tight-lipped unconcern.

The Government was now hoist with its own petard. Moore had landed at Oporto too late to be involved in the infamous 'Convention' and, on 27th September, Castlereagh wrote to inform him he was to command the Army in Spain and Portugal. Moore received the letter on 6th October, and before leaving England he informed the Duke of York that the officer he wished to have as his second-in-command was Sir David Baird. The precise reasons for his choice are not certain. Sir Charles Oman describes them as personal friends, though there is little evidence of this. But Moore had been impressed by what he had seen of Baird in Egypt and knew he was the only British General in the War to have successfully disembarked an army and marched it into enemy territory.

The two had much in common. They were Scots and dedicated soldiers with reputations as trainers of men and as intrepid leaders in action. Both had suffered from the patronage system and were distrustful of politicians. All these factors could be expected to ensure harmonious relations in the months ahead. But one important difference should be noted. While Baird had experienced supreme command on two occasions, this was Moore's first. There were also fundamental strengths and weaknesses in the characters of the two men that the campaign on which they were about to embark would ruthlessly expose.

When Baird arrived in Cork to take command of his troops, he was acting again under the orders of Castlereagh. His instructions were to embark the troops (seven battalions of infantry and two companies of artillery), and tell the naval commanders he was ready to sail. If the transports for the horses had not arrived, he was to sail without them.

Such a piecemeal start to the expedition went against his experience and instincts and, as he soon discovered, not only were there no horse transports but none for his artillery. Determined not to sail without his guns, he managed by a series of excuses to delay his departure until the transports arrived. He then sailed, reaching Falmouth on 28th September.

There, to his amazement, a letter from the Transport Board ordered him to send on his artillery companies to Plymouth. He dashed off a message to Castlereagh suggesting there must surely be a mistake by the Transport Board. On receipt of this, Castlereagh seems to have suddenly become aware of Baird's prevarication when at Cork. Incensed, he drafted a stern reprimand.

> "In the hurry of my last despatches I omitted to take notice of your having taken upon yourself to postpone the sailing of your corps from Cork, notwithstanding my express orders to the contrary. I am to desire that you will not, hereafter, take upon yourself to disobey an order which it is not in your province to consider yourself competent to judge."

Baird, however, remained in ignorance of Castlereagh's annoyance, though the affair must have added to his reputation for 'bloody-mindedness' among politicians. Having vented his irritation by writing the letter, the Minister seems to have had second thoughts. He was admitting to having allowed Baird to procrastinate. He had already antagonised Moore. Would it be wise to antagonise his Second-in-Command as well? Presumably reacting to such considerations, he decided not send the letter and ordered his secretary to send another which read:

> "Lord Castlereagh requests you will not stay for deficient vessels — they can follow. There was no mistake as to the artillery companies ordered from Cork to Plymouth; other companies are destined for your corps."

It is here worth noting that, while Baird was obviously guilty of insubordination, as a military leader he was right in refusing to be 'separated from his guns' — a point which coming events would amply demonstrate.

He now received his instructions and what to expect when he arrived at Corunna, his port of disembarkation.

Major-General Broderick, the senior officer on the spot, was arranging for the reception and 'comfortable accommodation' of the troops which Baird was to disembark immediately. Moore would be sailing from Lisbon to join him and the whole force of 30,000 infantry and 5,000 cavalry would be cantoned in Galicia until equipped to take

THE CORUNNA CAMPAIGN 1808-9

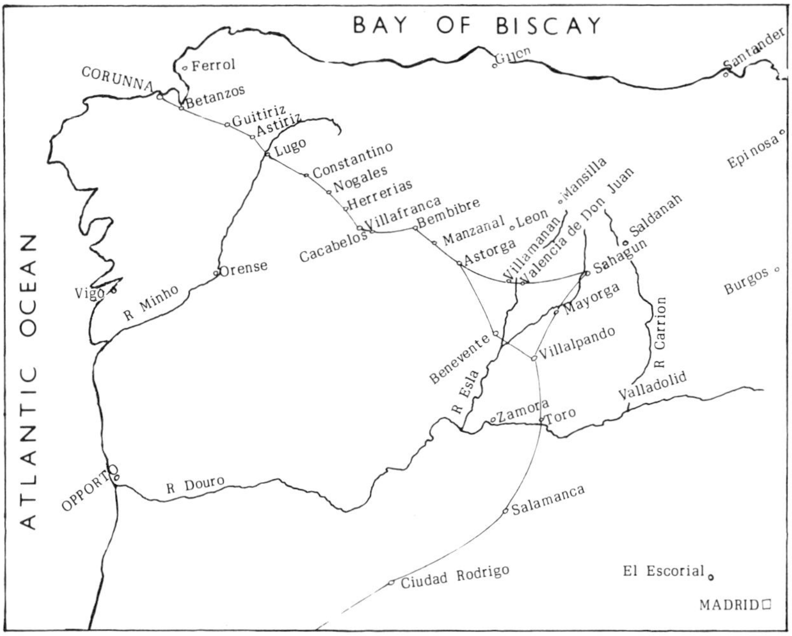

the field. Transport for the army would be laid on by a commissary, Mr. Affioti, who was already in the Asturias collecting horses and mules. Baird was enjoined to be strictly economical when purchasing supplies and to pay in Treasury Bills wherever possible.

Business-like and straightforward as all this sounded, Baird had too much experience of politicians' plans and promises to accept them at face value. But as he stepped on board *HMS Loire* on 6th October, he was expecting to serve under a leader after his own heart and one that might be relied on to solve any problems that might arise. He had with him his nephew, Captain Gordon, as one of his aides and Captain Sorell who had been with him at the Cape as his military secretary. His Generals, Major-Generals Manningham, Warde, McKenzie and Brigadier-General Craufurd embarked on other men-of-war.

The voyage was smooth with but one incident of note. On 12th they passed a division of Juno's army returning to France. Under the provisions of the Convention of Cintra, they were sailing in British ships and would soon reappear on the battlefields of Spain.

Next morning the fleet sailed into Corunna, described at the time by Crabb Robinson, the *Times* correspondent, as 'a little town in an out-of-the-way corner of Spain'. Its crescent shaped harbour could hold a large fleet and looked impressive. But on inspection, Baird found several disadvantages as a military port. The Atlantic swell came sweeping in; contrary winds could effectively lock ships inside or outside the harbour, both harbour and town were dominated by hills from which enemy artillery could make the place indefensible.

He was soon diverted from such considerations. No General Broderick appeared and enquiries revealed that he had left Corunna for the Asturias before Castlereagh's instructions arrived, so that preparations for the troops' reception had not even begun. Baird went ashore and, through an interpreter, made a formal request to the Galician Junta for permission to disembark his troops. He was told that a Supreme Junta had just been established at Madrid to handle such matters. As a local body, they had no power to sanction so important a move. His best course would be to sail on to Gijon or Santandar.

The stark reality that Castlereagh and the Government had been completely misled as to the true facts of Spanish resurgence was now evident. Far from welcoming a British army, the Galicians positively resented its presence. A situation to tax the wits of any general, for Baird it held exceptional difficulties. His experience of war had been almost entirely in India. He knew no Spanish and little French. He had no official interpreter and days passed before he could find an officer 'with sufficient knowledge of the Spanish language to act in that capacity'.

But as McGrigor had said, he was a man least liable to panic and, as usual, this had a calming effect on those he was dealing with. He explained to the Junta that he could not possibly leave Corunna unless ordered to by Sir John Moore or the British Government. Meanwhile there were two ways they could help. They could send a courier to Madrid for permission to disembark his troops and they could allow the horses to come ashore.

The Junta agreed to these requests. The same day Baird wrote to Moore announcing his arrival, adding with characteristic understatement, that 'an unexpected difficulty' had prevented his compliance with instructions to land the troops and send on the transports to Lisbon. But as soon as permission came from Madrid, he would lose no time in carrying them out. His letter concluded: "Permit me to express the sincere satisfaction and pleasure I experience at being appointed to serve under your orders.'

He was being noticeably formal and remained so until Moore's letters began to arrive and set the intimate tone of their correspondence over the next two months.

By 15th, the horses and wagons were ashore, landing places for the troops had been decided on and 850 wooden houses inspected and approved as billets, but that was all. Supplies, even bread and fodder for the horses, were almost impossible to come by. This, Baird realised, was partly due to real shortages. The Provinces had been milked almost dry to equip the army of General Blake, Commander of the Spanish Army in the North of Spain, now in the Asturias.

There was also the problem of payment. On the assumption they would be waiting for him at Corunna, Baird had brought neither money nor paymaster. They were not. And with the Junta making it plain that they were interested in hard cash not Treasury Bills (bits of paper), he had to appoint a commissary as temporary paymaster and ask him to raise £25,000. After strenuous efforts, the man came up with £4,800 at well above the going rate for the Spanish dollar. In desperation, Baird appealed to Castlereagh, to Moore and to the Consul in Oporto for help.

His first letters to Moore display a faith in his superior's knowledge of the situation. On 15th, he asked him to send his Quartermaster-General and Deputy Adjutant-General because the officers he had in these departments were so inexperienced. Next day he wrote privately to Moore, urging him to come to Corunna as soon as possible to direct operations before the army took the field, giving as his reasons his ignorance of the Government's intentions, of the country in which they were operating and his 'want of knowledge of the Spanish and French languages' when dealing with the Junta.

By 17th, after four days' dogged perseverance, he was slightly more optimistic. He had got General Muller, a senior officer at Ferrol (the nearby naval base), 'a most intelligent officer', to act for the Spanish Government. Muller had suggested that Moore should land at Vigo instead of Corunna as its facilities were better. Enclosing a list of cantonments at Vigo provided by the Spaniard, Baird concluded with the hope that 'we shall shortly see you here, when you will, of course determine the plan it will be proper to adopt'.

This was the first reference to Vigo which, from now on, Baird preferred to Corunna as a military port, a factor that would play a significant role in the campaign.

On 19th, two VIPs arrived from England. The first, General Romana, leader of the Spanish force that had been serving with the French and had escaped from Denmark in British ships, was drawn from the quay in a flower-bedecked coach to the Town Hall amid scenes of wild jubilation. The *Times* correspondent thought Romana looked like a Spanish barber and, in spite of the sneer, this was a shrewder assessment than that made by the politicians at home who saw him as a symbol of Spanish resistance. The warm reception to the other arrival, John Hookham Frere, the newly appointed ambassador to Madrid, was not unconnected with the £500,000 he was bringing for the use of the Supreme Junta.

For Baird, their reception compared with the one he and his men were receiving must have been galling, but the presence of so much money at least cast a ray of hope. He approached Frere and was reluctantly given £50,000 and permitted to beg another £25,000 from the Galician Junta, which, with their share of the British donation to the Spanish war effort in mind, they graciously granted. Greatly relieved, Baird immediately paid his officers their allowances and the men their month's arrears of pay.

Next day the first of Moore's letters, written on 12th, the day before Baird reached Corunna, arrived.

> "I need hardly say the satisfaction it afforded me when I found I was to have you as my colleague," it began. Then came the shock news. He was not coming to Corunna but was marching his army out of Portugal to Burgos by three separate roads and would join Baird 'at some intermediate place'. Baird, meanwhile, should 'place his troops in the most convenient cantonments in and around Corunna and take steps for the immediate equipment of them to take the field'.

To Baird, the irony of these instructions was obvious. But from the moment he knew that Moore would not be joining him and that the fate of his contingent was in his hands, a marked change in his reactions to events is apparent. No general needed less to be reminded of the dangers threatening the wings of an army, widely separated and open to attack by a more powerful enemy. From now on his overriding concern was to see that his wing would not be caught unawares.

On 22nd October the courier returned from Madrid. His despatch, read out to the Junta by Mr. Frere, permitted the British to land at Corunna if sailing on to Santander was not practicable. But the men must disembark in parties of 200 to 300 and be sent on into Castile without equipment or draught animals. At this Baird dug his heels in.

To forward his men in small detachments would court disaster. If the Spanish armies to his front were defeated (and from his observations of their troops at Corunna he had formed an accurate estimate for their chances against the French), his army would be destroyed piecemeal. Until he was allowed to quarter and equip his troops in and around Corunna, they would remain on board until he received orders to the contrary from home or Sir John Moore.

For a time the Junta held out. But from their nine days experience of Baird, they realised that, if they wanted to get rid of his 10,000 troops, they would have to give in.

On 24th, Baird informed Moore that his men would disembark and be cantoned in the towns and villages on the two main roads to Leon and Castile while they were being equipped to take the field. On 26th, the men, a third little better than recruits, began to come ashore. Cooped in the transports, having existed on ships' rations for almost two months, the effects on their health, discipline and morale are incalculable.

Now began the impossible task of equipping them from local resources, either non-existent or deliberately withheld. In a letter to Charles Stuart in the Madrid Embassy, Baird pointed out that before any action could be taken it had to be referred to a 'Junta composed of a dozen persons, some of whom throw obstacles in the way of every measure that is suggested'.

Yet he refrained from condemning the Spaniards, pointing out that they could not be transformed from enemies into allies overnight and that they had good reasons for their 'backwardness'.

> "They distrusted our intentions and suspected us of a design to seize the arsenal at Ferrol. Two or three officers who rode over to the place,

> were refused permission into the town; and a division of Spanish troops which was on its march from the south to Galicia to join Blake, was suddenly ordered to retrace its steps for the purpose of garrisoning and securing the fortress."

Nothing had been heard from Mr. Affioti, supposedly collecting transport animals in the Asturias and all that had been obtained locally were 5 mules. It was apparent that if a junction with Moore was to be achieved, the troops would have to move out with light equipment and under their own resources.

CHAPTER 16

Spain. The advance to Sahagun. 1808.

The three regiments of the Light Brigade under Craufurd were due to march on 27th with a bare minimum of equipment. As a foretaste of things to come, torrential rain fell and at the last moment the contractor refused to deliver the provisions he had promised. The reactions of the fiery Craufurd can be imagined though, under Baird, whom he had known years before in India, he appears as a model of subordination. He moved out the next day in slightly better conditions, the Brigade, wrote Crabb Robinson, "forming their Battalions to the sound of a very war-like description and marching off in the best of order."

The following night relations with the Spaniards touched crisis point. In a letter to the Horse Guards, Baird reported that Ensign Cartwright of the 1st Guards had publicly insulted the Governor and Mayor of Corunna and nearly provoked a fight between the British and Spanish Guard. His report concluded:

> "As, however, it is evident that his violence was solely imputable to madness and that he is altogether unfit to continue in the service, the only means that could be adopted was to confine him and send him on board."

Another matter of concern was the non-arrival of the cavalry. Due to a series of shipping hold-ups, the first did not arrive until 8th November when Lord Paget sailed in with the 10th Dragoons, two troops of artillery and the wagon train. Next day came 500,000 dollars, according to Castlereagh for Baird's exclusive use, though a month later the Treasury indignantly denied this. The rest of the cavalry arrived on 13th, the same day as Baird set out for Astorga. He travelled by coach, a sure sign that he was not the fit man, proud of his athleticism in earlier campaigns.

The Astorga road, intended as the supply route for the entire army, ran for most of the way through mountainous country with steep hills flanked by precipitous gorges. Along the 130 miles, in a single line were marching men, cavalry and guns, wagons and every type of vehicle, every horse and mule that could be bought or hired, hauling and carrying vast quantities of stores and ammunition from the ships at Corunna. At each town on the route, a detachment had to be left for security and to keep up the flow of supplies. Arrangements were, of necessity, hurried and makeshift. Orderly progress was impossible, as each accident and breakdown brought the whole line to a chaotic halt.

Ominous signs of indiscipline appeared. Young Captain Gordon of the 15th Hussars, placed in charge of a number of troops that were catching up their regiments, found them insubordinate and contemptuous of the NCOs. He was greatly relieved to hand them over.

In his efforts to enforce discipline, Baird found himself impeded by a strange oversight by Moore. When three dragoons were convicted of 'outrage and robbery', he decided to make examples of them only to discover that the Warrant for Courts-Martial Moore had sent him, omitted to allow him to carry out the sentences.

In Portugal, meanwhile, Moore had also been having problems equipping his troops. Yet, in spite of Baird's explicit accounts of his difficulties at Corunna, he continued to believe they must be of a local nature and that when the whole army entered Spain it would receive the whole-hearted support of the Spanish Government and people.

He had divided his army into four divisions, sending them by different roads to ease the strain on the resources of the country. Three, under Beresford, Fraser and Edward Paget, were routed for Salamanca via Ciudad Rodrigo or Almeida. But because of bad reports on these more direct roads (mistaken as it turned out), he had sent Sir John Hope with his artillery, his only regiment of cavalry and a body of infantry on the road to Madrid. Hope would be marching on a line roughly parallel with the other divisions until he reached El Escorial on the outskirts of Madrid. He would then have to turn sharply and march North West almost 100 miles to Salamanca.

With 70,000 Spanish troops reportedly somewhere along the line of the River Ebro, holding back any French reinforcements, the move had seemed safe enough. Yet, as Moore realised, he was committing the 'most unmilitary act' of separating himself from his guns — for which Baird had been prepared to incur the displeasure of Castlereagh before leaving Cork.

Moore left Lisbon on 26th October, the day Baird's troops began to disembark. He rode via Abrantes and Almeida and at Ciudad Rodrigo, his first stop in Spain, the first shock of disillusionment with the Spanish war effort began to fill his mind with foreboding. He unburdened himself to Baird.

> "I wish we were once united and that our commissaries knew how to feed us, and that the Spaniards were more firm and decided; for whilst

> at Madrid they are wrangling and all the generals are separate and independent, we can look for nothing but disasters, if the French are in sufficient force to move forward. However, we must hope and do for the best."

He reached Salamanca on 13th November, to be greeted with the news that massive French forces were moving into Navarre and Old Castile and had even entered Burgos, the point on which he was hoping to advance when his divisions were united. But with Hope at El Escorial and Baird not yet at Astorga, he was separated from his two most important divisions by almost 200 miles and their junction was no longer certain.

Neither by experience nor temperament was Moore prepared for such a predicament. His reputation was based on success as a divisional commander, on his enlightened work with his own Regiment and his training of the light infantry at Shorncliffe, (an elite body of men, 'intelligent, hardy and active'). At Shorncliffe he did not favour much drill and encouraged his men to talk openly when questioned. He is reported as saying: "Soldiers were always good if they were kindly treated, but officers were hardly ever good, never minding their profession, but devoted to eating, drinking and getting away to Balls."*

Sensible as these views appear today, he was faced with the stark reality that most of the men he had now to command were of a different calibre and trained in quite different conditions to those at Shorncliffe. Equally, his views on officers, correct in many instances, were not likely to bring out the best in them in the days ahead.

In his youth, during his travels through Europe with his father and the Duke of Hamilton, Moore had often led a solitary existence and had 'learned to keep his own counsel'.* Now, at Salamanca, he retired into himself, refusing to discuss his problems with others or to take advice. He devoted much time to writing — to Castlereagh, to Frere at Madrid, to Baird, to the Spanish generals, to his family and friends and in the diary which he had kept for years. His voluminous correspondence, which dwells much on how he had been misled into taking the army into its present dangerous position and blames the Spanish leaders for their lack of effort, appears to have served as a release for intolerable tensions. As to plans for the future, his mind ran on two alternatives and was closed to other suggestions. If the enemy permitted, he would combine his forces and 'do his duty' to

*_The Creevy Papers_ Edited Sir H. Maxwell. (1912).
†_Sir John Moore_ by Carola Oman.

the Spanish people; or he would retreat.

It was ironic that Baird had not only led two successful expeditions but was now placed where he could acquire far more knowledge of what would soon be the main theatre of operations. Because of this and his habitual caution taught by hard experience, his letters show a clearer and more detached view of events.

On the road to Astorga, he received news that daily increased his concern for the safety of his division. At Lugo, he heard of the defeat and dispersal of Blake's army at Epinosa. If the French followed up their victory, his left flank would be exposed to an attack from the Asturias. No less alarming were the indecisive letters arriving from Moore. In the first Baird was asked to 'push on' his troops from Astorga to Benevente. In the next he was warned on no account to 'commit in any degree' the safety of his corps.

On 16th, Moore feared he would himself have to fall back on Ciudad Rodrigo and told Baird to be ready to retreat on Corunna. Yet in another letter of the same date, he thought Baird should collect his whole force at Astorga and be ready to join him. The next day he was even hoping to assemble his army between Salamanca and Zamora and wanted Baird to send 'a considerable part of his force' to Benevente. As each of these letters took several days to arrive, Baird could form no clear idea of Moore's location or intentions at the time he received them. But when he reached Astorga he had made up his mind on one thing: no help would be forthcoming from the Spanish armies and it was up to the British to see to their own safety.

He wrote to Moore that, for him to make a partial advance to Salamanca at the moment would be to invite the piecemeal destruction of his division. By 29th he expected to have a regiment of dragoons, the horse artillery, three brigades of six-pounders and some infantry with him. He could then advance with some degree of security. If, however, Moore wanted him to send what troops he already had, he would do so instantly, adding:

> "I beg to assure you my dear Sir John, that in every instance, and on every occasion, it will be my anxious desire to meet your wishes and views."

These short extracts sufficiently reveal the conflict between loyalty to his superior and the need to ensure the safety of the 13,000 men now under his command.

Receiving no further letter from Moore, he wrote on 21st, repeating his assurances and making the startling admission that he was without spare ammunition. He also gives the first indication that he was turning to the practical details of a retreat:

> "I have despatched engineer officers to the rear for the purpose of ascertaining what impediments to the enemy we might occasion by the destruction of bridges &c in the event of being hard pressed and compelled to fall back on Galicia."

Two days later, still with no word from Moore, he began to fear that their lines had been cut and that Moore had been forced to retire on Ciudad Rodrigo. In this extremity, he called a meeting of his generals. Exactly what was said is not recorded, but presumably Baird set out the extreme dangers they faced and his plans to meet them. If there was any dissension it does not appear in the document that was drawn up and signed by all the generals present, whose names are sufficient testimony to Baird's powers of persuasion. They were: Lieutenant-Generals Baird and Paget, Major-Generals Warde, Bathurst and Broderick and Brigadier-General Craufurd.*

After the meeting Baird wrote to tell Moore of his concern at not receiving any letters for four days. He explained that because of the dangers to which he was exposed following the defeat of Blake, he had consulted his General Officers 'as to the measures it would be proper to adopt' and had found their sentiments were 'perfectly in union with his'. These were that it would not be advisable to attempt any advance until the whole force was assembled, which would not be before 4th December. If the enemy advanced before then he would instantly commence his retreat, 'taking care to move by the time they were three days march of me, to prevent the confusion and loss necessarily attendant on a close pursuit'.

Having thus foretold the future with uncanny accuracy, he went on to forecast (correctly) that the remaining Spanish armies under Castanos and Palafox could well 'have met with the same reverse as Blake; in which case the Spaniards could have no force deserving the denomination of an army in the field'. He then put in a nutshell the decision that Moore would have to make.

> "As it could never be intended by the British Government that our army should engage in the defence of this country unaided and unsupported by any Spanish force, I confess, My Dear Sir John, I begin to be at a loss to discover an object at this moment in Spain."

*The document is among Baird's papers in the Scottish United Services Museum. It was evidently not sent to Moore.

From his letters and diary it is clear that, militarily, Moore agreed with Baird. But unfortunately for him and his army, he was under political pressure from the Junta at Madrid and the fanatical devotion to the Spanish cause of Frere, the Ambassador. He was also inhibited, in a way that Baird would not have been, by 'What will they think at home?'.

This is shown by his indecision on what course to take. On 26th he seems satisfied with what Baird and his generals had decided and wrote: "Whatever you do, I am certain will be right, and I shall approve." Two days later, while castigating the Junta:

> "They deserve to be hanged, for it is owing to their imbecility that this country is unprepared." he still thought "it is our business to make every effort to unite here to aid the Spaniards as far as lies in our power — it would never do to retreat without making the attempt."

What form this attempt should take he did not say and probably did not know. Baird had no doubt and on 29th he offered 'a few ideas and remarks on his observations and the intelligence he had received'.

If the army were to unite, (as Moore had suggested), between Astorga and Salamanca, he foresaw two dangers. The French were in sufficient strength in the North of Spain to take the city of Leon, push past Astorga and take control of the passages into Galicia. The British escape route to Corunna with all their accumulated supplies would then be lost.

What, he asked, would be the objective of the army if it were united? If it was to move forward, might that be just what the enemy wanted? Their object would then be a fixed one — "the annihilation of the British army with immense means, or forcing it to make a precipitous and disadvantageous retreat."

The question was how the army should be placed to avoid these disasters? The answer, he suggested, was for Moore, by a flank movement to join him on his right at Astorga. From that position the line of the River Esla, which he believed to be strong, could be held for a time. But if the enemy advanced in great strength, 30,000 British troops, assisted by the Spaniards, could fall back on Galicia where, supplied from Corunna, they could probably defy the efforts of the enemy. It should be carefully considered before all these advantages were to be given up by the British. For by so doing they could well be walking into a trap which the enemy was preparing for them 'with a long hand'.

Time would show the wisdom of this advice. But unfortunately, just as Baird concluded his letter, he was handed one from Moore that at once threw everything into the melting pot.*

Castanos and Palafox, just as Baird had forecast, had been routed. No Spanish army now existed. Napoleon had 80,000 men in Spain with 30,000 more expected. Moore was about to retreat on Portugal. Baird must fall back on Corunna, first sending back the stores, but delaying at Astorga as long as he thought safe in order to deter the enemy from attacking the rest of the army. From Corunna he was to sail for the Tagus. He must write at once to England for transports to be sent to Lisbon to evacuate the whole army, 'for when the French have Spain, Portugal cannot be defended'.

These orders are typical of Moore's pessimism, which was to affect the whole campaign. He could not visualise a defensive war either in the Galicias or in Portugal, where Wellington later successfully based his operations. Having decided to retreat, he called together his generals and announced his decision. In contrast with how Baird had handled the subject days before, he made no attempt to take them into his confidence. Briefly announcing his intentions, he told them he took full responsibility and was not soliciting advice. All he required was they should carry out his orders promptly and efficiently.

Whether this was a demonstration of Moore's strength of character, as his admirers have asserted, or an admission that he lacked the capacity to carry his generals with him, must remain an open question. But the effect on discipline and the morale of his officers is not in doubt. All spoke openly against the decision and even his personal staff did not try to hide their disappointment.

A few days later, Frere in Madrid, although in no position to judge the military situation, charged Moore with betrayal of the Spanish people and tried to exert improper pressure on him to change his mind. At the same time he did suggest, as Baird had done, that Moore should move towards Astorga where he could take up a strong position and, if necessary, fall back on Corunna.

Baird at once gave orders for the retreat to begin, though the magnitude of the task has never been fully recognised. Troops, guns, wagons, carts, horses and mules carrying provisions for the whole army were stretched in a line from the ships at Corunna to the storehouses at Astorga. With all this having to be set in reverse, some chaos was inevitable.

Before leaving Astorga on 4th December, he published an address to the Spanish people, thanking them for their warm reception and

*Although his letter was not sent, Baird repeated his suggestions in the later one.

assuring them the British intended to reassemble at a point where they could more usefully serve the Spanish cause. He also despatched a letter to Romana, urging him to fall back on Galicia where he could collect his men and resources in safety.

Arrived at Villa Franca, he set up his HQ in the Castle to co-ordinate the retreat and begin working out plans to 'throw up entrenchments on the heights and maintain a position until Blake and Romana had recruited their armies'. Several observers, including Captain Gordon of the Hussars, thought this a wise move as the town was 'at the entrance of the strong mountain passes which continue almost without interruption for 12 leagues'. Against resolute resistance it would be impossible for any army to advance.

A week after the retreat had been ordered, Baird received a letter reflecting a new indecision on the part of Moore. The people of Madrid had taken up arms and were refusing to surrender to the French. Admitting he did not believe the insurrection stood a chance, Moore had received a formal request from Frere to support it. Baird was to suspend his retreat.

"All this appears very strange and unsteady," Moore concluded. Yet one wonders if he fully realised the effect the reversal would have on the troops and supplies now in full flow back to Corunna. Next day came positive orders; Baird was to 'put to the right about and return bag and baggage to Astorga'. Whatever the outcome of the Madrid rising, Moore had decided, the British must be at hand if needed 'whatever the risk'. He would 'proceed bridle in hand; for if the bubble bursts, and Madrid falls, we shall have a run for it'.

Once again, Baird's columns were put into reverse at incalculable cost to the final outcome of the campaign. Some of the troops were on their last lap to Vigo and had to march the 100 miles back to Astorga. But it was not the sudden change of plan that most concerned Baird. It was Moore's intention of advancing into the very jaws of the enemy.

In his reply he stressed again the advantages of the combined army covering Galicia and part of Leon rather than exposing itself near Salamanca. If Moore would join him at Astorga, it was 'his confident belief that they could cover the country to their rear while waiting to see how the Spaniards reacted. They could be reinforced from Corunna. They would not want for food as the country abounded with cattle, while flour for bread could be brought from England. By controlling Galicia they 'would furnish a rallying point and act as a stimulus for the Spaniards'.

His advice passed unheeded. At Salamanca, Moore was formulating a very different plan. He would unite his army and, in co-operation with Romana, advance to Valladolid and perhaps to Burgos to cut the enemy's communications.

His reasons for acting on a plan so fraught with danger are hard to understand, for it was clearly against his own military judgement. This is shown in a letter he wrote to Frere: "I not only risk to be surrounded every moment by superior forces but to have my communications cut with the Galicias."

Apart from this he had received solid evidence from one of Baird's officers that nothing could be expected from Romana.

Days later, he knew that Madrid had fallen and Napoleon's full might would be turned against him. Yet still he pressed on. His objective would no longer be Valladolid. A letter from Napoleon to Soult at Saldanah was brought to him by some peasants who had murdered the officer carrying it. Soult was instructed to take Leon and advance on Benevente and Zamora with his two divisions. He could do so with impunity, the letter read, as the British were in full retreat to Portugal. Moore, assuming (wrongly) that Soult was also ignorant of his position, decided to strike a surprise blow to dislocate the enemy's plans. He would collect his forces and advance on Soult at Saldanah.

His exchange of letters with Baird, though still cordial, now show how wide was the gulf in their views, for up to the moment they were joined, Baird did his best to persuade his superior not to risk the defeat and loss of his army. On 10th he suggested once again that Moore should join him rather than leave Galicia open. On 12th he wrote from Benevente to warn Moore that, if he intended to defend Galicia, he should concentrate his forces in defensive positions as soon as possible. He warned of the calamities that would befall an army in a forced retreat. The roads would be blocked with snow; Romana's men could get in the way, exhaust the country and 'consume the magazines'.

Moore, though still determined to advance, was looking to his escape route with increasing anxiety. He thanked Baird for his opinion about the Galicias and the use of Vigo as the port of embarkation, which he would probably use 'should such a measure become necessary', and he was anxious that 'magazines should be formed on that communication'. On 14th and 16th he again urged Baird to take every measure to form magazines on the road to Corunna, 'for though we may do something here, we must always look for a retreat on Galicia'.

He was asking the impossible. Even as he wrote, Baird had reached Benevente and was no more in a position to alter the arrangements than Moore himself. On 19th, the two generals met and shook hands at Villapando. Next day their two forces joined at Mayorga. Five days before, Baird had accepted Moore's invitation to command a division rather than remain as second-in-command with none. He could well have done so with relief since Moore had been so impervious to advice.[6]

But now Moore was at least carrying his army with him. After weeks of marching and counter-marching, the troops had the scent of action in their nostrils. Pains and hardships forgotten, they marched in high spirits along the road to Sahagun. And there, on 21st December, after one of the most brilliant cavalry charges of the whole Peninsular War had been carried out under Lord Paget, Moore set up his HQ. The men had outmarched their supplies and for a day, impervious to snow and freezing fog, they were content to rest and prepare for battle.

As dawn broke on 23rd, a thaw had set in. But all was ready for the attack and hearts were high. The River Carrion had first to be crossed and Baird's division was drawn up in columns to move along the road to the bridge at the town of Carrion. He had mounted his horse and was about to give the order to march, when he was handed a message telling him to go at once to see Moore.

A letter had just arrived from Romana. It said that Napoleon was aware of their present position. He had ordered the French army marching on Lisbon to counter-march and was himself coming from Madrid by forced marches with an overwhelming force.

The bubble had burst. Moore was caught in the trap against which Baird had so desperately tried to warn him.

Orders went out at once to commanders to inform the troops the attack was off. Baird broke the news, telling his men to go to their quarters and prepare for a retreat. The effect was shattering. "From the greatest pitch of exaltation and courage, all ranks were plunged into solemn gloom," said one of those present. "Nothing was heard on every side but the clank of firelocks thrown down in despair which before they had guarded as their greatest treasure."*

See Appendix 6

*Captain Sterling, 42nd Royal Highland Regiment.

CHAPTER 17

Spain. Retreat to Corunna. 1808.

The River Esla, which Baird had proposed as their first line of defence, became the first obstacle to be crossed. From their present position, one main road ran north to a bridge at Mansilla, defended, it was hoped, by Romana's men; another ran south to a bridge leading to Benevente and this was the route to be followed by the main army.

Baird's division was directed to an intermediate ferry-crossing near Valencia de Don Juan. In near zero temperature, pouring rain and a biting wind, at times knee-deep in mud, his 8,000 men, with their wretched train of women and children, made their gloomy way to within sight of the river, where, in the same cheerless conditions, they passed Christmas night. By dawn the river was rising at an alarming rate. It would obviously be impossible for so many to cross in daylight by the only available barge. A little lower down-stream, a ford was discovered and there Baird directed the main body. Watched by anxious groups on either bank, parties of men, women and terror-stricken children, pack-horses, mules and donkeys, cursed and yelled at by their Spanish drivers, struggled through the fast flowing waters.

The level continued to rise until at last the ford had to be abandoned. But it had served its purpose. By the end of the short winter's day, just as the last men were ferried across, pickets from Junot's army, released under the Cintra Convention, were starting to appear on the other side.

Posting strong parties at the River crossing and ordering camp to be set up in and around the small town of Villamanan, Baird sent a letter to Romana, urging him to blow up the bridge at Mansilla to delay the advance by Soult on Astorga. For the next two days he held his position to allow time for the other divisions to cross the bridge to Benevente and be on their way to Astorga. On 29th he was on the march again. At Obijos he came upon the rear guard of Romana's men. They had fled at the approach of Soult's pickets and left the bridge at Mansilla intact. Near to nudity, without arms, ammunition or food, they were preparing to join their comrades in Astorga.

At dusk, Baird's men reached the city. Exhausted after the day's march of 20 miles, they were met with a scene of utter confusion — the streets filled with men from Hope's and Fraser's divisions, some drunk, some wandering about to find a resting place for the night — the scarecrow remnants of Romana's men intermingling with ani mals, guns, wagons and broken-down carts of every description. With great difficulty, a scanty supply of food was obtained for Baird's men and it was late when he retired to his HQ at the Episcopal Palace which also housed the Brigade of Guards.

With no information to go on, the army still clung to the illusion that the next day would bring the longed-for action. But before dawn the order came to continue the retreat. On Moore's orders, the magazines with ammunition, entrenching tools and every type of equipment and clothing were set alight. As the flames leaped into the sky, punctuated by tremendous explosions, the army's resentment flared. Instead of fighting the enemy their leaders were marching them to death. They were even being denied the right to march; for men in some units were already without shoes, while tens of thousands of pairs were going up in flames. There had already been insubordination and crime, but from this stage, observers agree, the British were no longer an army but a rabble.

After the briefest of rests Baird's division was again on the march. In the rear of Hope and Fraser, its units were constantly being infiltrated by stragglers, while their own were in the greatest danger of being cut off by the enemy. Unlike the rear-guard under Sir Edward Paget, they had none of the morale-boosting excitement of brushes with the enemy.

By the evening, they had reached a village where they hoped to pass the night. Bread had been obtained at Astorga but in the haste and confusion of the advance, the commissariat had been able to issue it to only a few men. Some bullocks were now slaughtered and, until checked, the cabins of some of the wretched villagers were taken as fuel. Many men tried to shelter from the cutting wind and snow in the lee of buildings, beside banks and in hollows. They had no sooner settled when orders came from Moore, with the rear-guard to begin the march to Bembibre, 12 miles away. Much time and trouble was expended before all the men could be rounded up. At 10 o'clock they were on the move again, most still fasting as there had not been time to cook the meat.

At dawn they reached Bembibre, capable of holding only a third of the army. Doors had been barred by the terrified citizens. Many were battered down and the cellars raided. As Baird's division arrived, an orgy of destruction and drunkenness was already under way. It roused the men's flagging energies and many joined in. The stay in the town lasted only a few hours before the arrival of the rear-guard signalled the order to march. Many failed to respond, the drunk hiding in the wine cellars, the exhausted in any corners they could find.

They were kicked and prodded into action by Paget's men while those too drunk were left to their fate.

Hours later as these stragglers stumbled out of the buildings, a body of French cavalry rode through the lines of men, women and children, 'slashing among them as a schoolboy does among thistles'. A few of these mangled wretches managed to catch up with the main body at the next stop. Moore ordered them to be paraded along the lines of troops as a grim warning to the rest. It was a futile gesture. "Our commanders are worse than the French: will they not let us die in peace if they cannot help us," was typical of the comments from the ranks.*

At Villa Franca on New Year's Day, the scenes of rioting were repeated. Although there were ample supplies of food, the haste of the retreat made it impossible for it to be distributed in an orderly manner. Baird's division, the last to arrive, found much of the food had been taken or wasted.

Next morning, Moore had the whole army paraded. In an impassioned speech, he condemned the disorders, branded the stragglers at Bembibre as drunken cowards and hoped he would be killed by the first cannon-ball rather than survive the disgrace they had brought upon him. His speech was wasted on men who had lost all faith in their leader.

In sharp contrast, back at Cacabelos, a young major-general, Edward Paget, was crushing the seeds of rioting that had appeared in his rear-guard. Forming the five regiments into a square, he made them witness the systematic flogging of their comrades 'caught in the act'. The floggings continued up to the moment the enemy came in sight. The lesson was learnt; most of Paget's men survived to cover themselves with glory.

Baird was hoping Moore would adopt the same remedy. He sent his military secretary, Colonel Sorell, to ask him to call a halt for a time to re-establish discipline and if possible make a stand, for it will be recalled that Villa Franca was the place he had selected as the strong point to defend the passes to Corunna. It would be better, he suggested, to lose some men in action rather than risk destroying the whole army in so frantic a retreat. Moore thought otherwise and the divisions moved on.

As the last of Baird's men left they could see going up in flames the vast quantities of supplies, including food, that had been brought with so much effort from Corunna. And now it was no longer the

*_A Soldier of the 71st_. Anon. Known only as Thomas.

worst elements that were falling out by the way. Fatigue, starvation, despair and the elements had reduced all to the same level. In the words of Thomas of the 71st:

> "Dreadful as our former march had been, it was from Villa Franca that the march of death may have said to have begun. From Villa Franca to Castro is one continued toil up Monte del Cabero. There was nothing to sustain our famished bodies or shelter them from the rain or snow. Fuel we could find none. The sick and wounded that we had still been enabled to drag with us were now left to perish in the snow. The road was one line of bloody foot-marks from the sore feet of men; and on its side lay the dead and dying. Human nature could do no more."

Captain Gordon recalled with bitterness the General Orders in which Moore blamed the conduct of the troops on the 'inattention and neglect of the officers'. How could officers perform their duties, he asked, when they were subjected to the same sufferings and privations as the men?

His view is supported by a voice from the ranks. Thomas saw Guards officers plodding along with pieces of sacking wrapped round their feet and legs while the men found malicious pleasure in holding them up to ridicule.

"There goes a thousand a year!"

"There goes the prodigal son, on his return to his father!"

Generals and senior officers, many well into middle age were suffering extremes of exhaustion. General Anstruther had dysentery, was unable to mount his horse at Betzanos and died on reaching Corunna. General Manningham did get back to England but never recovered from the fatigues of the retreat.

Even Baird's iron constitution was affected and some of his reactions were becoming out of character. At Corunna, he had given Moore his reasons for thinking Vigo a better port for embarkation than Corunna. The Navy thought so too as, at Vigo, they could anchor out of range of any shore fire. At Astorga, Moore had agreed and had sent his light infantry, under Craufurd and Karl Alten of the German Legion, via Orense to where all the transports were waiting at Vigo.

But on 3rd January, at Herrerias, he received reports from his engineers that convinced him the march from Lugo to Vigo was too far. He wrote to the Navy ordering the transports to sail for Corunna and sent his aide, Captain George Napier, with despatches telling the divisional commanders to halt at Lugo where he was hoping to make a stand.

Napier rode through the dark 'in a heavy storm of rain, sleet and snow' to arrive at Nogales where Baird's division had stopped for the night. Taken to Baird's quarters he was annoyed to find him and his aide, Captain Gordon still in bed and 'not thinking of moving although day was broke'.

After reading the despatch, Baird asked Napier if he had been ordered to take the one to General Fraser or was he to forward it. Napier replied he had only been ordered to deliver it to Baird, but if no officer was available he would take it.

Baird said, "Oh, no. If you are not ordered to go, I shall send it by an orderly dragoon."

Napier repeated that although not ordered, he was willing to go, as he knew the message was 'of consequence'.

Baird cut him short with: "Sir, that is my business. I shall send it by a dragoon."

Napier withdrew and a dragoon was sent. The man 'overfortified himself with drink' and lost the message. The loss was not discovered for several hours and another message had to be sent.

Napier says that, although Moore was annoyed, he said little when he saw Baird. But Graham, his volatile aide, was extremely angry and expressed his opinions openly before the two generals. How far Napier's account is accurate is impossible to say. For reasons that will appear later he carried a life-long grudge against Baird and did his best to present him in a bad light.

Baird did not try to defend his actions and there can be little doubt that, for the first time in his life, he was losing grip on a military situation. This was partly from exhaustion and was perhaps increased by the belief that the frantic speed of the retreat was not necessary.

His reaction to the arrogant young Napier, who came upon him at an unfortunate moment, was hasty. But if Napier had received no orders from Moore, Baird would have been loth to send him on with the message. And although unwise after the event, his decision to send a dragoon was militarily correct.

The incident is of further interest. Moore's staff, at first disaffected by his decisions, were closing ranks to defend their chief against the open criticisms by the rest of the army for his handling of the retreat. Even in the case of the drunken dragoon, no blame was being attached to Baird. Gordon blamed Moore's 'vacillating conduct' for Fraser's having to be recalled, while Beresford, who commanded a brigade in the division, was incensed at having to counter-march. He thought that having gone so far on the road to Vigo, he should have been allowed to continue.[7]

His divisions collected, Moore decided on 7th January to make a stand at Lugo. The army responded with a remarkable return to order and discipline. On 8th they took up a strong position and waited throughout the day. Then, as it became clear that Soult could not be drawn into attack, Moore gave orders for the retreat to be resumed. The decision was inevitable. He had neither food nor other supplies for a long stand. In a few days, Soult could out-flank him by the track roads to the north. For the British to attack would invite annihilation and even a victory could not be exploited.

But the army knew and was told nothing of this. The night saw one of the worst storms, ensuring again the rapid destruction of discipline. At 9 o'clock, in pitch darkness, with rain and hail driven by gale force winds, the first divisions started to move on. An hour later, Baird's followed. He rode, as usual, in the rear to superintend the routing out of stragglers not only from his own division but the many others who had given up in despair and sought shelter from the storm.

In the first light of day it was seen that only a small advance had been made. Groups of men and even whole units had wandered through the night in circles on the rocky mountainside. The Commanding Officer of one unit came up to Baird in great distress to report that he could not find any of his men, so inextricably mixed were they with other regiments.

A brief halt was called at the village of Valmeida. Some of the men had been told to stay in their ranks and lie in the mud to rest. Others, out of compassion by their officers, were allowed to seek whatever shelter they could find. Baird, the last to arrive, told his men to do likewise. An hour or two later, when the drum signalled a resumption of the march, many who had taken shelter refused or were unable to respond. How many of these may have expired in the mud as did some of their comrades, or how many rejoined their regiments later, cannot be estimated.

It now became the rule to start off each regiment with its colours even though only a fraction of the men were present, the task of rousing up those who had hidden themselves or dropped from exhaustion falling on Baird, his brigade commanders and their staffs. At Betanzos, 12 miles from Corunna, the whole army stopped for the day. Miraculously the depleted ranks began to fill again, a sure sign that the pursuers were now suffering like the pursued. The rest of the way was down hill and for the first time the sun shone. A degree of

See Appendix 7

orderliness began to return, but only the thought of food and home kept many on their feet.

The transports had not yet sailed in from Vigo but were hourly expected, and rest in a quiet haven was all that mattered.

It was 15th before the transports finally came. The wounded, the women and children, the troopers and the artillery were taken on board. Thousands of barrels of ammunition had been exploded and the cavalry horses were slaughtered, in what was, for some, the most ghastly sight of the campaign.

By the morning of 16th, plans were well under way for the orderly embarkation of the infantry. But before they could be removed from their defensive positions on the hills surrounding the bay, four enemy columns preceded by skirmishers were seen advancing down the hillside.

Baird's division occupied a position to the right of the line where the main assault was expected. As the French columns approached, Moore rode up to Baird who asked if it was not time to advance and whether Moore would give the word. Moore replied:

"No, Baird. Do you."

They were the last words exchanged by the two generals.

The order was given. Moore moved away. A few moments later Baird was struck by a charge of grapeshot on his left arm within an inch of his shoulder. Another blast tore a hole in his side. Although stunned, he managed to dismount. As his mind slowly cleared he tried to remount. Finding it impossible, he was persuaded by an aide to retire from the field. His arm supported by his sash, he walked the two miles back to his quarters in the town, his face and manner so normal that several officers he passed had no idea he was wounded.

He was taken on board his ship where the surgeon, finding him composed, said cheerfully that he would 'soon have him to rights'. His self-control momentarily lost, Baird asked the man angrily if he thought he would have left the field for a trifle.

Investigation showed the bone of his arm smashed to pieces with splinters so near the shoulder that the usual form of amputation was impossible. Told his arm would have to be removed from its socket, Baird expressed doubts but was assured that, if his life was to be saved it had to be done. At the suggestion that he must be exhausted and the operation deferred to the next day, he replied he was ready for it to be carried out at once.

The amputation, an unusual one at that time, was performed with Baird seated with his right arm resting on the table. He remained impassive until the final separation of the arm from the joint, when 'a single exclamation of pain escaped his lips'.

As the dressings were being applied, Sorell, his military secretary, came. Baird received him 'in his usual affectionate manner' and, giving him his remaining hand, said how pleased he was to see him alive and well. When told of the death of Sir John Moore, he was moved to tears. But being assured the battle was running in England's favour, he said he would have to resign the command to Sir John Hope. He was then laid on a camp bed and given a powerful opiate (laudanum).

Next morning, he awoke in command of his faculties and, finding the British victory confirmed, sent his nephew to ask Hope for a detailed report of the action. On receiving it, he told Sorell to write a letter to the Secretary of State to accompany it, shakily adding his signature and telling Gordon he was to have the honour of taking the despatch to London.

While within regulations and obviously to advance his nephew's career, by reassuming command, Baird had set the cat among the pigeons. At least two of Moore's staff, Major Colbourne and George Napier, as well as some of Hope's, thought they had a prior claim to carry the despatches. Napier was not willing to give up the honour. He tried to persuade Hope and Graham to 'remonstrate' with Baird, though whether they did, considering the state he was in, is doubtful. Gordon was not too happy about having the honour thrust upon him for he did remonstrate with his uncle, only to be told:

"If you don't go I shall send Captain Baird."

Gordon apologised to Napier and went.

Hope, an unspectacular but reliable general, did the sensible thing. He sent a duplicate despatch with Colbourne, who arrived in London a few hours after Gordon.[8]

The voyage home proved a fitting epilogue to the Campaign. The transports with their cargoes of wounded, ragged, emaciated, lice-ridden men were struck by storms. Two foundered on the Cornish coast, with the loss of 270 men. In the ceaseless tossing and clamour of the ship, Baird suffered dreadfully from his wounds and the delayed shock of the operation. The faithful Sorell tells of how 'his mind constantly dwelt on the events of the campaign' and how, at times, he had to be restrained from attempting to get up to perform his duties to his men.

When the ship berthed at Plymouth, hearing that his old friend Dr McGrigor was based at Portsmouth, Baird requested to be taken there by sea. He arrived on 25th January, his fever abated and in good

See Appendix 8

spirits, though the boisterous weather prevented his being brought ashore.

On 27th, his brother Joseph went on board with Dr McGrigor to see him and 'at noon he was lifted ashore in a large cot normally used for swinging ladies on to the ship'. He was carried by several of the crew to a house in the High Street.

> "His landing," wrote McGrigor, "excited much attention, mutilated as he was by the loss of a fourth of his frame. The lower class of people, of whom there was a great assemblage, showed the greatest respect towards him, mixed with strong marks of feeling: all admired his manly, soldier-like bearing, although his face was wan."

Sir John Moore had died in the hour of victory and was buried on the ramparts of the Citadel at Corunna. His heroic death, lovingly recorded by devoted friends, has erased from history the responsibility he bore for the disasters of the Campaign.

His 'wipe at Soult' they acclaimed as a stroke of genius. But most who suffered the horrors of the Great Retreat said it was never worth the risk and that, as Baird had constantly urged, he should have looked to the safety of his troops and retired to Galicia after Madrid had fallen. He was saved from complete annihilation by Romana's letter. Had that failed to arrive, he would have crossed the River Carrion and Soult was too astute a general to have given battle. He would have drawn Moore on until the trap set by Napoleon had closed. Then, not a British soldier would have escaped.

CHAPTER 18

Scotland. Indian Summer. 1809 — 1829.

Baird's convalescence lasted a long and tedious year on a small estate in Hertfordshire, with an occasional visit to London. He was awarded the KB, ten years after Mornington first recommended him for it, and in April reluctantly accepted a baronetcy. At the ceremony he met his old friend Lachlan Macquarie, who was being presented to the King on his appointment as Governor of New South Wales.

By summer 1810 his health had improved and on 4th August he married Miss Ann Campbell Preston, a Scottish heiress with a large estate at Crieff in Perthshire. Of how they came to meet we know nothing and of the lady very little except that she was strong-willed, an impression reinforced by Raeburn's portrait done at the same time as the one of Baird, now hanging in the Hydro at Crieff. He may have unconsciously found someone in his mother's image, for he accepted her domineering with a touch of stoicism. Once, after she had got her own way, he observed wryly:

"I could command 10,000 men; yet I cannot command one woman."

The early years of marriage were divided between London and Crieff where their mansion, known as Ferntower, was being enlarged. In May 1811, Baird sat on a court-martial at which Colonel Johnstone, the Lieutenant-Governor of New South Wales, was charged with leading a mutiny against Governor Bligh. Of Bligh's not surrendering to the troops sent to arrest him (he was found hiding under a bed), Baird remarked that this was what any sensible man would do in the circumstances. Writing to Macquarie, now in the hot seat from which Bligh had been removed, Baird regretted being absent the day sentence was passed, because of an operation on the wound in his side. He believed this was fortunate for Johnstone, as he had 'never heard so connected an evidence proving him guilty of mutiny without the least palliative that was to my mind worthy of consideration'.

In London in the summer of 1813, he was posting a plan of the extensions to Ferntower which had been requested by Mrs. Macquarie, when he learnt that George Molle, his military secretary on the Egyptian Campaign, now commanding the 46th Regiment, was about to sail for New South Wales as Lieutenant-Governor. 'Friend Molle' he imagined, would be a great acquisition to Macquarie.[9]

See Appendix 9

About the same time, he met John Malcolm for the first time since leaving India. According to Malcolm, Baird came up to him 'with open hand and heart' and, after recalling how bitterly he had complained at Wellesley having been 'put over his head', he said:

> "It is the greatest pride of my life that anyone should ever have dreamed of my being put in the balance with him. His fame is now to me a joy, and I may say, glory, and his kindness to me and mine has all along been most distinguished."

The kindness was probably Wellesley's having taken his nephew, Captain Gordon, as one of his aides. In fact the choice had been on merit. Wellesley not only regarded Gordon as one of the best but, when he was killed at Waterloo, was moved to tears.

After the defeat of Napoleon in 1814, the Peninsular Generals Hope, Hill, Graham, Beresford and Stapleton Cotton (though not Picton, disliked by Wellington for his outspokenness), received peerages and pensions of £2,000 a year. Persuaded by his wife and friends, Baird sent in a list of his services with a claim for the same reward. He received no reply.

Towards the end of the year, Ferntower was ready for occupation and there Baird found great contentment. All his trophies were given a prominent place — the swords, the relics, decorations and, in a place of honour, the straight-backed chair his mother had used. Only one important memento was missing — the shirt woven by John Lindsay in their long captivity, had been left in his abandoned coach at the start of the retreat to Corunna,

With improving health, absorbed in running the estate, he was on horseback every day and was even boasting he could shoot as well with one arm as he had ever done with two. Freed from financial worries he could indulge in the pleasures of open house though, sadly, his old friend James Robertson had died that year. The paternal attention he had paid to his soldiers he now transferred to the tenants, the old stern sense of duty mellowed into active concern for the poor.

From time to time, he applied for Government appointments but without success until 1819, when he was made Governor of Kinsale and the following year was given command of the army in Ireland. The reason for the Government's change of heart can be guessed at. After the War, indiscipline amongst regimental officers that reached such heights of folly under the Earl of Cardigan was much in evidence. There was need for a firm hand in charge.

He took with him to Dublin his old colleagues Sorell, as his secret-

BAIRD IN RETIREMENT

Courtesy: National Portrait Gallery, London.

ary, and Middlemore as his chief aide. At least one regiment regretted his appointment. Its officers had taken a whore into their mess. The regiment was posted to India. Sir Walter Scott, whose son was in the regiment, thought Baird had done the right thing but was concerned for the health of his son in that far-off land.

With civil disaffection rife he had to try to resolve the age-old Irish problem of assisting the Government to keep order while preserving the discipline and efficiency of the army. He held office until June 1822, when the establishment was reduced for economy reasons, the post of C-in-C being abolished and replaced by a Head of Staff.

His letter on handing over has a sadly modern ring. One local rising had been put down and no outrage had occurred since. But there were still large numbers who,

> 'although deficient in leaders of rank and influence, entertain designs hostile to the Government and the present order of things; and act under the obligation of an oath that binds them to secrecy and mutual support. - — - the nature of the service in Ireland exposes the military to many privations and much fatigue, and to a dispersal which, in a worse constituted army, would prove fatal to discipline..'

He was greatly moved by the conditions in which many Irish people were living and detailed the terrible distress in some areas brought on by a potato famine. In Galway, 'hundreds of half-famished wretches arrive almost daily from a distance of 50 or 60 miles; many of them so exhausted by want of food, that the means taken to restore them fail of effect from the weakness of the digestive organs occasioned by long fasting'.

On his retirement to domestic life, he received letters from Sir Robert Peel, the Home Secretary and from the Duke of York, highly commending him on the way he had carried out his duties. Few of his oldest comrades now remained. John Lindsay, the last survivor of their captivity, had gone. Macquarie, returning from Australia in 1821, a sad and disappointed man, had been a frequent visitor to Ferntower. On the anniversary of Seringapatam in May 1824, he and Baird with the dwindling company of those who took part assembled to drink the usual bumper. Two months later Macquarie was dead.

Baird was himself slowing down and, unlike his old self, not averse to solitude. A pathway from the house led to a secluded spot commanding a magnificent view of the surrounding countryside. On a rustic seat beneath a beech tree, he would sit and think over old times: the trials and disappointments, the happiness and success.

Sometimes he would be joined by a young man, curious to hear tales of the past.

In 1827, an article on the Duke of Wellington in *Blackwood's Magazine* commented that, in the conquest of Seringapatam, General Harris had been assisted by a Military Council and 'that of the members who composed that Council, without whose sanction no important matter could be undertaken, Colonel Wellesley was one'.

Harris, now 81 but still ready to defend his reputation, indignantly denied such a Council ever existed. He claimed to have exercised full authority and had 'great satisfaction in remembering that upon Sir David Baird requesting to be relieved from the government of Seringapatam, which he had nobly earned, the successor whom I appointed as the ablest of the able, in my opinion, was the present highly welcomed Commander-in-Chief of all his Majesty's forces.'

Baird smiled wryly, but refused to correct Harris' distortion of history.

The same year, Sir Walter Scott published his *Life of Napoleon*. Highly critical of the British at Corunna, he asked why Moore had not fought a defensive war in Galicia instead of advancing against the French. In October, Sorell wrote a long letter to Scott, pointing out how Baird had brought to Moore's notice many times the advantages of falling back on the mountain passes in Northern Spain. Scott did not bother to reply.

In 1828 appeared the first volume of William Napier's classic History of the War in the Peninsula. While eulogising Moore, it was severely critical of Baird. Sorell, 'actuated solely by considerations of public justice and private friendship', replied with Notes on the Campaign of 1808-9 in Northern Spain, giving a full account of the part Baird had played in the Corunna Campaign and countering all Napier's criticisms.

Baird must also have been concerned, for he sent Sorell's Notes with a covering letter to Wellington. He received the following reply:

> "My Dear General,
> I received your note and the Tract enclosed last night; and I will read the latter immediately.
> But I assure you that I have not read one word of Sir Walter Scott's *Napoleon* excepting the first Volume, or of Col. Napier's book.
> Ever Yours Most sincerely,
> Wellington."

There was no further communication between the two.

Early in that autumn, Baird was riding towards home when his horse fell with him. He was badly hurt but managed to remount and reach home. He made light of the accident and appeared to stage a recovery. But the shock and injuries from the fall to a one armed man now in his 72nd year, took their toll. A few weeks later he suffered a sudden attack of giddiness, followed by a bout of sickness.

Under the care of his old friend Dr McGrigor, he was nursed back to a state where he was able to take a lively interest in events and on 23rd April was well enough to attend a levee on his appointment to the Governorship of Fort George, a belated gesture of goodwill by the Government. A few days later, he had an attack of excruciating pains in the head which continued intermittently over the next months. In July, he was taken home to Ferntower, where he calmly set about arranging his affairs. He suffered a relapse on 10th August and died on 18th.

He was buried near Crieff, though his body was later taken to Culross to be reinterred at the burial place of his wife's family. In 1832, Lady Baird had a monument to his memory erected on a hill known as Tom-a-Chastel on her estate. An exact replica of Cleopatra's Needle, it still stands though now hidden by tall trees.

Soon after her husband's death, Lady Baird commissioned the popular novelist, Theodore Hook, to write his biography. In two volumes, padded with much extraneous material, Hook's work was successful in that it exposed the injustices which Baird had suffered and, in particular, it raised a storm of controversy over his supersession after the capture of Seringapatam.

It is safe to say that Baird, never one to court publicity, would not have approved the disclosure of those long gone events. But Wellington, when asked by J W Croker, the gossip diarist, for his comments, no doubt reacting to the reminder of the supersession saga of more than thirty years ago, maintained he was the right man for the job and added:

> "Baird was a gallant, hard-headed officer, but he had no talent, no tact; had strong prejudices against the natives; and he was peculiarly disqualified from his habits, &c, and, it is supposed, his temper for the management of them.
>
> "Notwithstanding this, he and I were always on the best of terms and I don't think any man rejoiced more sincerely than he did in my ulterior success."

With few exceptions, Wellington's assessment of his one time rival has been accepted by the Duke's biographers. However, writers who recorded the achievements of British soldier heroes have been kinder to Baird's memory. Sir R T Wilson in his History of the Expedition to Egypt, (1803), compares the conduct of Wellesley and Baird at being superseded. Wellesley, he writes, displayed 'a degree of exultation' when he arrived at Baird's breakfast table in Seringapatam, whereas Baird, at Bombay, 'sensitive as a woman to the feelings of those in distress', was incapable of exulting over Wellesely's supersession.

J W Cole, in his British Generals distinguished during the Peninsula War, (1856) had this to say of Baird:

> "A warrior without fear or reproach, intending no guile and believing in no treachery. Throughout his long life he made many friends and never lost the esteem he once acquired. He was not given to talk of his own services and exploits and was ever ready to bear testimony to the deeds of others. He thought he had been treated with neglect and inadequately rewarded, but he rejoiced when his comrades were successful; and though his application for a peerage was passed over without the courtesy of an answer, he was never heard to insinuate that those preferred were not deserving."

From Edinburgh boyhood to landed gentleman at Crieff, the most remarkable impression of the man was how little he was changed by adversity; and how, in the pursuit of glory, the bonds of friendship and humanity held firm to the end.

END

APPENDIX

(1) The above account was given many years later by Baird to an officer who visited him in his home in Perthshire. Because of his reputation for gallantry a rumour was widely believed that when ordered to take over the command, Baird had pointed out to Harris how unfair it would be for Wellesley, a young officer at the start of his career to be deprived of the chance to redeem his mistake of the night before. On this Baird remarked that as any soldier must know, it would have been impossible for him to have hesitated or made any remark to the Commander-in-Chief of an army on receiving such an order. Any merit in delaying the attack, if indeed there was any, belonged to General Harris, not to him.

(2) It became almost proverbial in Mysore 'that Hyder was born to create an empire and Tipu to lose one'. The only quality the son inherited from his father was courage. In every other respect his powers and inclinations led him to failure. Father and son were unprincipled but where Hyder saw clearly the way and means to success, Tipu's vision was distorted by emotion and prejudice. Hyder was well served by men of all religions: Tipu would have none but Muslims and by oppressing his Hindu subjects he lost both their talents and allegiance. Hyder listened to others before making decisions; Tipu held council only to state his intentions and allowed no criticism. Where Hyder was moderate in success and always managed to salve some advantage from defeat, Tipu was intoxicated by success and despondent in failure. He spoke continually of *jehad*, holy war, but by faulty choice of leaders the efficiency of the army he inherited gradually declined. His final failure rose from his neglect of his cavalry, the arm with which Hyder had been able to defy the British for so long. Against Hyder in his prime, Harris' army would never have reached Seringapatam.

(3) George Elers begins his account: "With respect to the unjust affair of superseding poor Baird in the command at Seringapatam, I heard it from Colonel Wellesley's own statement in the apartment of the palace, the Dowlet Bagh, where the scene occurred. Colonel Wellesley said in his rapid manner of speaking: 'I went down to Baird one morning early . . ."

(4) McGrigor became Wellington's Chief Medical Officer in the Peninsula and not infrequently suffered from his uncertain temper and had to overcome the Duke's prejudices to maintain the health of the army. One example was when he took a personal decision to change the route of the wounded after a battle. Another was Wellington's refusal to introduce the French scheme of ambulances or to give Napoleon credit for his 'humanity' for using them. McGrigor's *Autobiography* was published in 1861.

(5) The Mamalukes evaded attempts at their extermination until 1811 when a great number were taken by a stratagem and massacred. The survivors were wiped out nine years later. As pawns in Power Politics their fate has a familiar ring in more recent times.

(6) Sir Charles Oman in his History of the Peninsular War finds the principles on which Moore rearranged his units hard to understand. Baird was given three regiments from Lisbon and had to pass over the Corunna units to Hope and Fraser. The regiments that had become accustomed to work together were thus separated. Moore may have intended to give each division regiments of varied experience?

(7) George Napier wrote his biography in 1828 'for the instruction and amusement of his children without any view to publication'. It was published after his death by his son. A forthright character, he is often unreliable on events and people. He made the most of Baird's being in bed but did not find out how long he had been there. He says 'day was broke'. Yet by his own account the time could not have been later than 5 am. In that part of Spain, the sunrise would have been about 8, and as it was a stormy night, there could have been no light before 7.30 at the earliest. (I am indebted for this information to the Observatory at Bidston).

(8) The account is taken from Napier. Still aggrieved when he arrived in England he appealed to Sir David Dundas, temporarily C-in-C the Army, (the Duke of York being under a cloud for allegedly allowing his mistress to traffic in the sale of commissions). Old Dundas, who disliked pushing young officers, told Napier he had nothing to complain about. Napier never forgave Baird and did all he could to injure his reputation.

(9) Molle had served well under Baird's firm control. But his arrival in Australia proved a disaster for Macquarie. He was soon intriguing with the Governor's opponents. The whole sordid affair was ended in September 1817 when Macquarie decided to order Molle on to a ship for England.

SELECT BIBLIOGRAPHY

Anon. *A Soldier of the 71st.* Republished Leo Cooper. 1974.

Blackwood's Magazine 1827. Wellington and Harris at Seringapatam. Article and letter.

Blakiston, J. *Twelve Years of Military Adventures.* 1829.

Cape Colony. Records of. Vols 5, 6, 7.

Bowring, L.B. *Haider Ali and Tipu Sultan.* 1893.

Chambers, R. *Traditions of Edinburgh.* Chambers. Reprint 1967.

Cole, J.W. *Memoirs of British Generals distinguished during the Peninsular War.* Vol 1.

Dictionary of National Biography.

Elers, George. *Memoirs.* Ed. Lord Monson and G. Leveson Gower. 1903.

Fortescue, Sir J. *History of the British Army.*

Glover, Richard. *Peninsular Preparations.* C.U.P. 1963.

Graham, H.G. *Social Life in Scotland in the 18th Century.* 1900.

Herald, J.C. *Bonaparte in Egypt.*

Hickey, William. *Memoirs.* Ed. A. Spenceer. 1923.

Hibbert, Christopher. *Corunna.* Batsford. 1961.

Hook, T.E. *Life of Sir David Baird.* 1833.

Ingram, Edward. *Two Views of British India.* Adams and Dart. 1969.

Keltie. (Ed). *History of the Scottish Highlands.* 1887.

Lindsay, John. *Seringapatam. Oriental Miscellanies.*

Elizabeth Longford. *Wellington. The Years of the Sword.* Weidenfeld & Nicolson. 1969.

Love, H.D. *Vestiges of Old Madras.* 1913.

Lushington, S. *Life of General Lord Harris.* 1840.

Macgrigor, Sir James. *Autobiography.* 1861.

Moore, Sir John. *Diary.* Ed. G.F. Maurice. 1904.

Munro, Innes. *Narrative of Operations on the Coromandel Coast.* 1789.

Napier, George, T. *Passages in the Early Life of.* 1884.

Napier, W.F.P. *The War in the Peninsula.*

Oman, Carola. *Sir John Moore.* Hodder and Stoughton. 1959.

Oman, Sir Charles. *History of the Peninsula War.* 1902-11.

Pearce, R.R. (Ed) *Wellesley, Richard Colley, Marquess.* 1846.

Pearson, Andrew. *Autobiography of a Peninsular Veteran.* Republished *The Soldier Who Walked Away.* Bullfinch. 1987.

Rajay, K. *History of British Diplomacy in Tanjore.* 1969.

Sorrel, T.S. *Notes on the Campaign in 1808-9 in the North of Spain.* 1828.

Thompson, E. *The Making of the Indian Princes.*

Thornton, L.H. *Light and Shade in Bygone India.* 1926.

Wellington. *Supplementary Despatches.*

Wilkie, Fletcher. *Recollections.* United Services Journal. 1836.

Wilks, M. *Historical Sketches of South India.* 1810-17.

Wilson, Sir R.I. *History of the British Expedition to Egypt.* 1863.

Wilson W.J. *History of the Madras Army.*